THE FUTURE OF INDIAN POLITICS

THE FUTURE OF INDIAN POLITICS

BY
ANNIE BESANT

GYAN

ISBN: 978-81-212-1894-8 (HB)
First Published, 1922
Published, 2018
Published by

Gyan Publishing House
5, Ansari Road
Daryaganj, New Delhi-110002
Phone: 011-47034999, 9811692060
www.gyanbooks.com
E-mail: books@gyanbooks.com

Printed at: G. Print Process, Delhi.

To the Aryan Motherland

and

To the coming World-Commonwealth,

To all Her Children,

white and coloured,

who have worked, suffered and died,

and—hardest of all—lived

for Her—

in love and loyalty,

in faith in her future,

Her Servant

lays at Her Feet this little book

FOREWORD

THIS booklet is intended to offer to those interested in the fate of India and Great Britain, a picture showing the problems that India has to solve in the near future in connection with Self-Determination and Self-Government, and in her decision between solitary Independence and Partnership in a Commonwealth of Free Nations, under the British Crown. The two last chapters deal with these; the background, necessary for the understanding and the decision of these two supreme questions, determining the future of both Nations, is painted in with care, so as to contain the vital facts, and those only, which have led to the parting of the ways, indicated in the problems. An Introduction gives " A Bird's-Eye View " of the relations between India and Britain, from their first important contact to the end of the East India Company Rule. "Step by Step" takes us from the first National Congress to the outbreak of the War. "A New Departure" tells of the Congress of 1914, Indians in the War, and the demand for the recognition of India as a component part of the Empire. "The Great Agitation" takes up the next two chapters, and carries us to the coming to India of the Secretary of State. "The New Spirit in India" marks the causes of her changed attitude. "The Struggle over the Reforms" tells of the Death of the Old Congress and the Reformed Legislatures. "The Revolutionary Movements" their causes and workings take us up to and through the Non-Co-Operation activity. Then follow the two last chapters.

I hope that the booklet may be useful in helping the understanding of the questions involved.

ANNIE BESANT

CONTENTS

INTRODUCTION

A BIRD'S-EYE VIEW

THE lives of India and England became interwoven on December 31, A.D. 1600, when Elizabeth of England gave a charter to "The Governor and Company of Merchants of London, trading in the East Indies". Then were linked together the destinies of the two Nations, though little did they bethink themselves of the wondrous tree that was to spring from that little seed.

The Portuguese were the first modern European Nation to come to India, for Vasco de Gama discovered the Cape Route, leaving Lisbon on July 8, 1497, reaching Calicut, on the West Coast, on May 20, 1498, and arriving again in Lisbon in August or September, 1499. Three years later, in 1502, he established the first European settlement in Cochin: Goa was taken in 1510, and became the capital of Portuguese India, and still remains under that rule. The French were next in the field, sending over men to report on trading opportunities as early as 1537, but she did not found any factories until 1668, when some traders settled down in Surat on the West Coast, and Golconda. The reports to the French Government of Bernier and Tavernier during the reign of Aurungzeb (1658—1707) are classical. The French "East India Company" was formed in 1664, but Aurungzeb deprived it of Golconda in 1687. The Dutch arrived in 1601, and established a "United East India Company" of their own in the following year; they built some factories on the East Coast, but finally devoted themselves to the conquest of Java and Sumatra, from 1649 onwards. Denmark followed next, and made a start with an "East India Company" in 1612, but her little earthen pot had no chance among the iron ones hurtling against each other, and she faded quickly away, leaving only some Protestant missionary centres in Southern India, and some traces also in Bengal. Ten years later, in 1622, the German Empire, then Austrian, started an "Ostend Company," and in 1644 Prussia made an experiment with her "Emden Company". But all these disappeared except the Portuguese, leaving France and England to battle, nominally for the trade with India, really for the mighty Empire, then but an embryo in the womb of the future. For the first English ships under the Elizabethan Charter had soon followed its granting, and in 1606 one reached Surat, and the traders began to look round. Meanwhile, a Captain Hippon started two trading establishments on the East

Coast, one at Pettapoli, and the other at Masulipatam. In 1612—or 1613, both dates are given—the East India Company made a serious beginning, for the Mughal Emperor Jehangir, son of Akbar, gave them a written document, permitting them to establish factories in Surat, Cambay, Gogo and Ahmedabad, and in 1616, the Zamorin of Malabar allowed them to set up a factory in Calicut, his capital city.

A glance at the conditions existing in India, during the sixteenth, seventeenth and eighteenth centuries, will show us how the stage was arranged by the Great Dramatist for the struggle of the French and English for the European control of India, the victory of Great Britain, for the swift and, down here, unplanned rise of Britain as the Head of an Indian Empire, the acceptance of its rule by two-thirds of the country as an immediate British Rāj (Kingdom), and the recognition of the British Sovereigns by the Indian

Monarchs, as Lords Paramount of India—in the traditional word, as Chakravarṭis.

This Overlordship was familiar as an incident in Indian history. When the Monarch of a State felt himself strong enough to claim suzerainty over his brother Monarchs, ruling the many Kingdoms into which the vast peninsula of India was divided, he sent out a White Horse to travel through the kingdoms during one year, and the guardians of the Horse demanded acknowledgment of their King as Lord Paramount of the whole of India, and tribute as a sign of that acknowledgment; if they met with refusal and the Horse was taken from them by a recalcitrant Monarch, they threw down the gage of battle, and war was declared. If the Horse was everywhere received with welcome, then he was brought back to his owner, the challenging Monarch, he was sacrificed with great pomp, and his Monarch was recognised as the Chakravarṭi, the Lord Paramount of India. The last Horse Sacrifice was performed by the Emperor Aḍiṭyāsena of the Gupṭa dynasty in the seventh century A.D. It was performed by Puṣhyamiṭra, the founder of the Suṅga Dynasty, in 148 B.C. Yuḍhiṣhthira performed it after the Great War, 3000 B.C. Before that, it goes back for uncounted years to Sagara, presumably accounted mythical by the short-sighted chroniclers of the West. It must be remembered that the Unity of India the "fundamental Unity," as Professor Radhakumud Mukerji calls it, has always been religious and cultural, and not political. This was untouched from the time of the successive Āryan waves of conquest, beginning about 18,000 B. C. and practically concluded by about 9000 B. C.—dates I give not from western "historical" documents but from the Occult Records, the "memory of Nature". (Hinḍū records place it much earlier, probably because they do not lay stress on the Indian and the pre-Indian Āryan Empires in Central Asia, Mesopotamia, and on the great Lemurian Continent. But this by the way. It is "another story".) This Unity was Āryan, and has a literature admittedly at least 7,000 years old. In this she is not known as "India," but as Bhāraṭavarṣha, Aryāvarṭa, Jambūḍvīpa; the great Emperor Ashoka, for instance, is called the King of Jambūḍvīpa. The prayers and hymns of Hinḍū rituals name her sacred rivers, her sacred cities, from Harḍvāra and Baḍarīkeḍār-nāṭh in the North to Kāñchi and Rāmeshvaram in the South, from Ḍvāraka in the West to Jagannāth in the East. This religious and cultural Unity, after existing for over sixteen hundred centuries, was broken, though but slightly, in the eighth century A. D. by the incursion into Sindh of Arabs from Bassorah, who had conquered Baluchistan, crossed the Indus and had settled down in Sindh, thereafter held by Musalmāns. A serious blow was struck at it by the Afghāns under the Sultān of Ghazni, in A. D. 986, and five centuries of struggle followed; in A. D. 1162, the Pathāns established themselves on the throne of Pṛiṭhvirāj, the last reigning descendant at Delhi of Yuḍhiṣhthira, and Babar, the Mughal, defeated the Pathān Sultān in A. D. 1526, and was proclaimed Emperor of India at Delhi, the founder of the mighty Mughal Empire, which also perished at Delhi in September, 1857, when the city was taken by the British under General Nicholson, who was killed in the final assault. The Theocracy of the Musalmāns caused a rift in the religious and cultural Unity of India, but Islām has added much to her Art and Science, and we will hope for a future synthesis of hitherto seemingly incompatible elements.

The immediate cause for the comparative ease of the British triumph lay in the rise of the great Marāṭha Power, preceded by a Hinḍū revival, and founded by the genius of Shivāji. He was crowned at Raipur in 1674 and died in 1680, but he had organised an Empire from Surat in the North to Hubli in the South, from the Indian Ocean in the West to Berar, Golconda and Bījapūr in the East. He had done more; he had "created a Nation". His younger son Rājārām, began the great twenty years' War of Independence, faced the Mughal army under Aurungzeb, left his nephew Shāhu to carry it on after his death, and Shāhu regained his grandfather's Empire. The "Marāṭha Confederacy broke the Musalmān power, established its five branches at Poona, Nāgpur, Indore, Gwalior and Baroda, and made the Great Mughal himself their puppet by 1803. They practically ruled India, but the struggles of Mughals and Marāṭhas had weakened their common Motherland, and into this welter came Britain and France, and played against each other for the great prize.

The two countries had increased in power during the rise of the Marāṭhas, without drawing much attention to their advances. England had founded Madras in 1640, obtained Bombay in 1662 as the bridal dowry of Catherine of Braganza, Queen of Charles II, and acquired Calcutta in 1698. France settled in Pondicherry in 1674, and established its government there. During this period, the great rivals intrigued against each other, playing for trade advantages with rival Princes, and helping one Prince or another with a view less of aiding the Prince than of weakening his antagonist, supported by the rival European Company. It was an underground war of rival traders. We need not delay on it, nor on the armed conflict which succeeded it. In the result, the English won, and looking below the surface, for those who believe in an Inner Government of the World, the reason was plain. I gave it in 1915:

> Britain succeeded, because she was the Power that held in her the most fertile seed of free institutions, because she was on the eve of establishing democratic government on her own soil on the surest basis, so that while she might enthrall for a time, ultimate freedom under her rule was inevitable. France had behind her then only the traditions of tyranny; the Bourbons ruled and rioted. India needed for her future a steady pressure, that would weld her into one Nation on a modern basis, that she might become a Free Nation among the Free. The High Powers that guide the destinies of Nations saw Britain as fittest for this intermediate and disciplinary stage. (*How India Wrought for Freedom*, Introduction, p. xxxvi.)

Let us remember these words, that "ultimate freedom under her rule was inevitable"; later, we shall see them proved.

I conclude this "Bird's-Eye View" by summing up the two main results one evil, one good, of Britain's rule in this country; the rule is divisible into two periods; the Government by the East India Company from the battle of Plassey on June 23, 1757, to the

Sepoy Rebellion in 1857, and the Government by the Crown from November, 1858, to the passing of the Reform Act in 1919. The first was wholly autocratic. The second slowly introduced elements of liberty, and in 1919 laid the foundations of Responsible Government.

The results of the first period were tragic beyond words. The Company had as its one object successful trade, the accumulation of wealth; there were several rival Companies competing for trade, but they were consolidated in 1702.

Here was a Company, to all intents and purposes independent; it was ruled by a Board of Directors in London; it chose its own agents, it made its own armies; after a time it appointed a Governor, then a Governor-General; it applied for Charters, for Courts of Justice, and got them—with subsequent horrors related by Macaulay. There was no effective control over its proceedings, although Parliament interfered for the first time in 1773, and a Board of Control was established in 1784, and the Court of Directors placed under it—a clumsy dual arrangement, making no real difference. The one useful thing was the renewal of the Charter, preceded by an enquiry, which at last revealed the state of things—and terrible are the records. When things became too outrageous, Parliament interfered, as in the impeachment of Warren Hastings; but, for the most part, Britain was far too busy with her own troubles, her loss of her American Colonies, her Napoleonic Wars, the struggles of her rising Democracy, the miserable condition of her people, her Chartists, her agricultural riots, and the rest, to trouble much about what a trading Company was doing in far-away heathen India; the Company made treaties and broke them, or forged them, if more convenient; it cheated, robbed, murdered, oppressed, and—built an Empire in about a century. Clive was the first Governor under the East India Company in 1758; Earl Canning the last in 1856. The Company ended in the Sepoy War of 1857, and the Crown assumed the sovereignty in 1858. (*How India Wrought for Freedom*, Introduction, pp. xxxix, xl.)

The results of the Company's rule during its first fifty years were summed up by Macaulay, who gives a terrible account of the oppressions of the Company at this time:

"Thirty millions of human beings were reduced to the extremity of wretchedness. They had been accustomed to live under tyranny, but never under tyranny like this . . . That Government, oppressive as the most oppressive form of barbarian despotism, was strong with all the strength of civilisation." He quotes a Musalmān historian, who praises the extraordinary courage and military skill of the English: "But the people under their dominion groan everywhere, and are reduced to poverty and distress. O God! come to the assistance of thy afflicted servants, and deliver them from the oppressions which they suffer." In 1770 there was an awful famine; "the Hooghly every day rolled down thousands of corpses close to the porticoes and gardens of the English conquerors. The very streets of Calcutta were blocked up by the dying and the dead." It was "officially reported to have swept away two-thirds of the inhabitants," (*Imperial Gazetteer*, ii, 480), or 10,000,000 persons. (*Ibid.*, xliii, xliv.)

The tremendous stream of wealth that flowed to England during this time gave the impetus to English industrialism that turned her from a Protection into a Free Trade Country, and made her, for a time, the greatest manufacturing country in the world. The result on India was terrible poverty and recurring famines; the latter chiefly due to the ruin of her industries and the consequent throwing of her population on the land; a similar ruin in Ireland had a similar result in famine, but there half her people emigrated to America; India had no such resource, so her people died where they were. Her poverty is still ghastly, as is shown by the average life of her population as given by Mr. Gokhale at 23·5 years; the average age in New Zealand is 60 years. I have written so fully on this (see Introduction to *How India Wrought for Freedom*, and many speeches in the body of the book; or, *India: —A Nation*) that I will not repeat it here; her present poverty is almost incredible, but stares us in the face by the slight hold the peasants have on life, as shown by the huge mortality from any epidemic, while her former wealth would be as incredible, were it not historically proved; and there is the significant fact that the Nations of Europe fought for her trade and the right to plunder her. Also her education was destroyed, and from being perhaps the best educated country in the world, with a "school in every village," she sank into an illiteracy greater than that of Russia. It is such facts, accumulated and circulated, which made our strength in the Home Rule movement, and won the Reform Act.

We submit from a review of this rough sketch:

That India, despite foreign invasions and local disturbances, which all Nations have suffered in their time—what peace had England from the Conquest up to the final defeat of Charles Edward in 1745?—was a prosperous and wealthy Nation before the coming of the East India Company, and that her huge wealth, down to the end of the eighteenth century, is a proof of general industry and security and immense industrial output among the masses, while the wealth of the merchants, and of the banking and trading communities shows a settled condition, where credit was good; that commercial integrity was so great that receipts and bonds were not demanded in financial transactions.

That the English connection, under the Company, reduced India to poverty, and dislocated her industries, and that, under the Crown, the Government still hamper her industries, make a cruelly severe drain upon the country, and by their fiscal arrangements prevent the return of prosperity. That between 1770 and 1900—130 years—there have been twenty-two famines, eighteen according to the Report of the Famine Commission of 1880 and four after 1880. In 1770, as we have seen, there was a famine in Bengal with 10,000,000 deaths; in 1783 in Madras; in 1784 in Upper India, which left Oudh in a pitiable condition; in 1792 in Bombay and Madras; in 1803 in Bombay; in 1804 in northern India; in 1807 in Madras; in 1813 in Bombay; in 1823 in Madras; in 1833 in Madras, where in one district, Guntur, 200,000 died out of 500,000 population, and the dead lay unburied about Madras, Masulipatam and Nellore; in 1837 in north India, in which a calculation of 800,000 deaths is thought too low by the Famine Commission; in 1854 in Madras; in 1860 in northern India, about 200,000 deaths; in 1866 in Orissa and Madras, in Orissa a third of the people died, about 1,000,000, in Madras about 450,000; in 1869 in north India, about 1,200,000 deaths; in 1874 in Bengal, over 1,000,000 were relieved and life was saved; in 1877 in Madras, 5,250,000 deaths; in 1878 in north India, 1,250,000 deaths; in 1889 in Madras and Orissa; in 1892 in Madras, Bengal and Rājputāna; in 1896—7 in North India, Bengal, Madras and Bombay—the number of deaths is not given, but 4,000,000 persons received relief; and in 1899—0, in north India, Central Provinces and Bombay, 6,500,000 persons were in receipt of relief—the worst famine on record. In 1892 and 1897, Burma also suffered from famine. In 1896, bubonic plague broke in Bombay, and has slain its millions. (*Ibid.*, pp. lii—liv).

The annexations, conquests, plunderings, only finished up with the annexation of Oudh in 1856, this last being the real cause of the Sepoy Rebellion, the last straw that broke the camel's back.

It is felt in India that her own system of Village Councils, and the ascending grades of which I shall speak presently were more successful than the new system imposed upon her, which turned her village servants into village tyrants; that her village industries and her many exquisite crafts have been well-nigh killed out by inferior cheap goods; that her irrigation, so carefully provided by her own rulers, has been starved, and forestry till lately disregarded, causing barren wastes and lessened rainfall; that British rule is costly, and has been too ready to resort to coercion where remedy of grievances should have been sought. But with the Reform Act she sees the dawning, and lifts up her head to greet the coming day. Let the dead past bury its dead.

What is the other side of the picture?

India's civilisation was based on the family, and therefore on "Ḍharma," mutual obligations. A man living in Society has duties to discharge, according to the faculties he brought with him into the world; in a civilised land, a man is born into a network of obligations. This theory gave her a stable social order, and her marvellous material prosperity and wealth, despite many raids, invasions, and local conquests by less civilised Nations; her vast area discounted the effect of these, and her agricultural and industrial wealth, her banks, her trade and commerce, remained with an unrivalled stability for at least 5,000 years, taking the date from ordinary western history. None the less, with the efflux of time, the sense of obligation, of submission to authority, grew disproportionately strong, and the earlier sturdiness of their Āryan forefathers slowly decreased; they became submissive to tyranny, and habituated to passive obedience. They looked on governing as the business of the governors, and if the governor governed tyrannically, it was for God, not for them, to remove him. Hence what might be called a political fatalism.

The English with their struggles for Freedom, their doctrine of human Rights, their rebellious independence and restless energy, equipped with the resources of modern science, their making their country the refuge of all western rebels against tyranny, and with an arrogant sense of their own superiority, were exactly the corrective for the undue submissiveness, the political indifference and lack of public spirit reigning in India. They gave external order after 1858, and, since 1835, they had been spreading English education, the beginning of which goes to the credit side of the Company, its only asset, except that they sent some first-rate men to India during the second quarter of the nineteenth century, and many of these inculcated English doctrines of Liberty. Macaulay in a famous passage, though in a tone of insufferable superiority, struck a fine note :

> It may be that the public mind of India may expand under our system till it has outgrown that system ; that by good government we may educate our subjects into a capacity for better government ; that having become instructed in European knowledge, they may, in some future age, demand European institutions. Whether such a day will ever come, I know not. But never will I attempt to avert or retard it. Whenever it comes, it will be the proudest day in English history. To have found a great people sunk in the lowest depths of slavery and superstition, to have so ruled them as to have made them desirous and capable of all the privileges of citizens, would indeed be a title to glory all our own. The sceptre may pass away from us. Unforeseen accidents may derange our most profound schemes of policy. Victory may be inconstant to our arms. But there are triumphs which are followed by no reverse. There is an empire exempt from all natural causes

of decay. Those triumphs are the pacific triumphs of reason over barbarism; that empire is the imperishable empire of our arts and our morals, our literature and our laws. *(India: a Nation*, p. 184.)

Mr. Dadabhai Naoroji said:

The introduction of English education, with its great, noble, elevating, and civilising literature and advanced science, will for ever remain a monument of good work done in India and a claim to gratitude upon the Indian people. This education has taught the highest political ideal of British citizenship and raised in the hearts of educated Indians the hope and aspiration to be able to raise their countrymen to the same ideal of citizenship. This hope and aspiration as their greatest good are at the bottom of all their present sincere and earnest loyalty, in spite of disappointments, discouragements and despotism, of a century and a half. (*Ibid.*, p. 64.)

He also pointed out that English Education was unifying India, and that political union was the first fruit of the awakening. Railways, posts and telegraphs made rapid intercommunion possible, and brought educated people into a sympathetic unity of ideas, aspirations and hopes. The revival of India's own religions, and researches into her long history aroused self-respect and gave birth to an intense pride in their Nationhood. The National Congress, largely inspired by Englishmen and by English ideas, focussed their aspirations and educated their hopes. Into such a Nation, thus prepared, swept the wave of a War based on Ideals of Liberty.

On all sides it is now admitted that the loyalty of the educated classes to the Crown and the Empire in this hour of sore trial has been perfect. How is it then that education has at once made them deeply resentful and yet loyal? The answer is very simple. English education has made them see the glory of English liberty, and they are passionately desirous of sharing it. English education has made them realise that they are the intellectual equals of Englishmen, and that even if they were not, they have exactly the same right to govern their own country as the Englishmen have to govern theirs. Hence English education has made them profoundly discontented with the autocracy of the Secretary of State, administered here by a haughty bureaucracy, whereof Macaulay said in prophetic words: "God forbid that we should inflict on her the curse of the new caste, that we should send her a new breed of Brahmins, authorised to treat all the native population as Pariahs." (*Speeches*, p. 73.)

But English education has also made them loyal, because they believe that the best realisation of their aspirations is in becoming a Self-Governing unit in the Federal Empire of which Great Britain will be the centre, and because they thus desire; they are fighting for that Empire to-day. (*Ibid.*, pp. 65, 66.)

Let us close on the note of the words that I said we should remember: "Ultimate freedom under her rule was inevitable."

CHAPTER I

STEP BY STEP

WE begin with the words with which we finished our "Bird's-Eye View": "ultimate freedom under her rule was inevitable"; and we must first note the great institution known as the Indian National Congress, which laid, well and truly, the foundations of Indian Freedom from December, 1885, to August, 1918, both in Bombay.

Some English critics, in the early days of the War, angrily declared that India had taken advantage of the War to press a new claim for Dominion status. That was not so. The new departure in 1913 resembled in one marked way the new departure when the National

Congress was planned in 1884. The seed of both was planted by the Theosophical Society. It was at the Theosophical Convention of that year that a small group of earnest Theosophists—deeply concerned for the political future of their country and aroused to a sense of her past powers and her then present impotence by the awakening crusades of H. P. Blavatsky and Henry Steele Olcott, stirring the educated to self-respect and respect for their Nation—meeting in Adyar, decided to make an effort for political redemption; feeble as they seemed, they felt strong in their belief that India's ancient Ṛṣhis still watched over Their ancient and ever well-loved land, and would aid their efforts to bring about her political resurrection; so they gathered a small meeting in Madras—there were only seventeen of them—and it was there decided to begin "a National movement for the saving of the Motherland" (*How*

India Wrought for Freedom, p. 2). A list of the seventeen is there given, quoted from the *Indian Mirror*, and they were mostly delegates to the Theosophical Convention from Calcutta, Bombay, Poona, Benares, Allahabad, Bengal, Oudh and the Northwest Province (now the United Provinces), and Madras. One of them, Norendranath Sen, Editor of the (Calcutta) *Indian Mirror*, says of them in his paper: "The delegates who attended the [Theosophical] Convention were most of them men who, socially and intellectually, are the leaders of the Society in which they move in different parts of the country." They resolved that on their return home, each would form a Committee in his own town or Province, and consult how to make their dream a reality. "In March, 1885, it was decided to hold a meeting of representatives from all parts of India at the then coming Christmas" (*Proceedings of the First Indian National Congress*). They estimated that seventy delegates would be present, and seventy-two attended, strengthened by thirty friends. From that first meeting in 1885 to that of Bombay in 1918—with one break-down at Surat in 1907—the Congress was truly National, and guided Indian Politics. During all these years the National Congress had awakened large numbers of the English-educated classes to political self-consciousness, and had trained them in political knowledge. English names, Hume, Wedderburn, Cotton, and others are found co-operating with the Indian patriots. It met yearly and demanded definite improvements in the system of Government, definite changes in legislation, definite reforms of abuses, definite limitations of autocracy and enlargements of liberty. In 1906, moved to anger by the Curzonian *régime*, Mr. Dadabhai Naoroji, as President, went beyond partial reforms, and declared that Indians should control India, as Englishmen controlled England. This was "absolutely necessary" for the progress and welfare of the Indian people.

> The whole matter can be comprised in one word, Self-Government, or Swarāj, like that of the United Kingdom or the Colonies . . . Self-Government is the only and chief remedy. In Self-Government lie our hope, strength and greatness . . . Be united, persevere, so that the millions now perishing by poverty, famine and plague, and the scores of millions that are starving on scanty subsistence may be saved, and India may once more occupy her proud position of yore among the greatest and civilised Nations of the West.

This clear note was drowned in the flood of anger which broke through all barriers at the succeeding Congress at Surat, and brought about the catastrophe of its breaking up, and a consequent tearing apart of the Congress party. The Congress thereafter resumed its method of pressing reforms piecemeal, until a new departure, linking itself to the declaration of 1906, was made in the Madras Congress of 1914.

Once more this was prepared for quietly, in a little meeting of Theosophists held in September, 1913, at Adyar, in which I told them of the need of a new move forwards for the fourfold regeneration of India, and asked their help. It was a "Conference of Theosophical Workers," called by me to organise more fully than previously the four lines along which National Regeneration must be worked for, if India is to take her rightful place as the spiritual teacher of mankind. Twenty years of Indian experience were behind me, and now the fourfold activity was to be consciously welded into one, and I called on the workers who had been pursuing with me one or other of these lines. They were reforms in (1) Religion; (2) Education; (3) Social Customs; (4) Politics; corresponding to man's fourfold constitution: (1) Spirit; (2) Mind; (3) Emotions; (4) Physical Body. In 1893, I had begun the work for (1) Religion against Materialism, continued ever since, so splendidly commenced and carried on by Colonel H. S. Olcott, taught and inspired by Helena Petrovna Blavatsky; he had worked most for Zoroastrianism and Buḍḍhism, both more congenial to him than Hinḍūism, though he served both it and Islām to a more limited extent; great was his rejoicing when he found that I was intellectually and instinctively Hinḍū, "to do for Hinḍūism," he said, "what I have done for Buḍḍhism". This inner leaning to one religion rather than another is, of course, the result of previous lives. In (2) Education, Colonel Olcott had chiefly confined himself to founding Buḍḍhist schools in Ceylon, and five Pañchama (outcaste) Free Schools in Madras, though he had also started many Bāla Samājas—Boys' Societies—for religious instruction, Government Schools in this country excluding religion from their curriculum, the only alternative being the Christian Missionary Schools, in which a faith hostile to the religions of the country is taught. In the education given by Theosophists, every student is taught his or her own religion—wherever possible, by a teacher belonging to it—and a common religious service opens each day in school. The restoration of Religion to its rightful place in Education has been a characteristic of all our educational work. After some years of lecturing on "National Education," I took part with other enthusiasts in founding, in 1898, the Central Hinḍū College and School in Benares, and we carried it on—giving an Education religious, intellectual, moral and physical (fourfold, as stated above), teaching loyalty to the Sovereign hand in hand with service to the country—until 1914; during these sixteen years, I was President of the Board of Trustees and Chairman of the Managing Committee. In 1914, we determined to give over our College and School, with its lands, buildings and funds to the Hinḍū University Society, of which we had become members, that it might be the nucleus of a larger work, and we elected from our Board its President and ten Trustees to be life-members of the Court, the University equivalent of our Board. Since then, we have served in the Court and Council, some of us in the Senate and Syndicate also, of the Hinḍū University. After I became President of the Theosophical Society, on the passing away of its President-Founder, Colonel H. S. Olcott, my place of residence became Adyar in the South, instead of Benares in the North, and in 1913 a Theosophical Educational Trust was formed there, which accepted students of all faiths in its schools; in 1917, came a Society for the Promotion of National Education, with Sir Rāsh Bihāri Ghosh as President, with which the Theosophical Trust affiliated itself, and this, with its University, of which Sir Rabinḍranāṭh Tagore became Chancellor and Sir Subramania Aiyer Pro-Chancellor, flourished exceedingly with, in 1918, six Colleges and many Schools, until Mr. Gandhi's movement spread hatred of all who did not accept his leadership, and lessened public contributions, forcing us to contract our work. In (3) Social Reform, the work for changing bad social customs went slowly in comparison with the preceding two, but within the Theosophical Society, we organised a band of Social Reformers, working especially against child-marriage—in the Hinḍū Collegiate School we gradually refused all married boys, taking a promise from the parents not to marry them while in the School—for the uplift of the submerged classes, for foreign travel and the extinction of outcasting as a penalty therefor. We also worked hard for Svaḍeshi—the use of Indian-made articles in preference to foreign-made—for Temperance, for the removal of caste distinctions in society by interdining and social intercourse, with intermarriage between subdivisions of the same caste, and for the removal of the colour bar between the white and coloured races in India and in all parts of the British Empire. For these things we formed a band of workers, united by a promise of practical work. In (4) Politics I worked more in England for the recognition of the Rights of India than directly in India itself, well knowing that until pride in India was aroused, pride in her past and hope for her future, until social self-respect and independence were awakened, no strong bases existed for true political liberty. Our Central Hinḍū College, at its outset, was branded as "seditious" by the Lieut. Governor, Sir Antony Macdonnell—now Lord Macdonnell, and still an enemy of Indian Liberty—and I was only saved from prosecution in 1910, by the strong intervention of

Mr. Gopal Krishna Gokhale, for an Appeal to Englishmen not to awaken hatred to their race by insulting treatment of Indians in railroads, restaurants, and other public places. The Anglo-Indian newspapers were furious, for I was very unpopular with the British in India, partly because I loved Hinḍūism and fought against missionary efforts to pervert Hinḍūs, especially schoolboys, and partly because I lived among Hinḍūs as one of themselves, sharing in their family life and observing their customs. For a white woman thus "to degrade herself," to be seen walking and driving with Hinḍūs, was anathema.

At the Conference of Theosophical Workers, these four lines of work were systematised in a small band, named "The Brothers of Service," and the following statement was drawn up, and circulated as a leaflet:

"Theosophy must be made practical" was a sentence written and published long ago by one of Those whom Theosophists regard as Masters.

Since Mrs. Annie Besant came to India in 1893, she has been seeking for ways of service to India, so that the country of her adoption might rise in the scale of Nations, and take the world-position to which her past entitles her and which her future will justify. Rightly or wrongly, she judged that the great Forward Movement must begin with a revival of spirituality, for National self-respect could only be aroused and the headlong rush towards imitation of western methods could only be checked, by substituting spirituality and idealism for materialism. Great success attended the work, and she then added to it educational activities, so as to appeal to the citizens of the future and shape their aspirations towards Nation-hood, as an integral part of the coming World-Empire. Cautiously she carried on some Social Reform activities, organising propaganda against child-marriage, and in favour of foreign travel, helping the latter by the establishment of an Indian Hostel in London,[1] and of a Committee of friendly Theosophists who would welcome youths arriving in England as strangers. For many years many of her more attached followers have been pledged to delay the marrying of their children for some years beyond the custom of their caste and neighbourhood. In Politics, she has urged the larger ideals, and has, especially in England, spoken for the just claims of India.

[1] This is an error; we only kept a register of lodging-houses with trustworthy landladies, and of private families where Indian lads would be taken as paying guests.

Now another step has been taken, and some of the best T. S. and E. S. workers enrolled themselves on the 20th September, 1913, in a band who have taken the following sweeping promise:

"Believing that the best interests of India lie in her rising into ordered freedom under the British Crown, in the casting away of every custom which prevents union among all who dwell within her borders, and in the restoration to Hinḍūism of social flexibility and brotherly feeling,

I PROMISE:

1. To disregard all restrictions based on Caste.
2. Not to marry my sons while they are still minors, nor my daughters till they have entered their seventeenth year. ('Marry' includes any ceremony which widows one party on the death of the other.)
3. To educate my wife and daughters—and the other women of my family so far as they will permit—to promote girls' education, and to discountenance the seclusion of women.
4. To promote the education of the masses as far as lies in my power.
5. To ignore all colour distinctions in social and political life, and to do what I can to promote the free entry of coloured races into all countries on the same footing as white immigrants.

6. To oppose actively any social ostracism of widows who remarry.

7. To promote union among the workers in the fields of spiritual, educational, social and political progress, under the headship and direction of the Indian National Congress.

Breach of any clause entails expulsion from the organisation. Those who are not prepared to take the whole of this, may take any clause or clauses which they feel they can work for. Thus some who are in Government Service, take all but 7, as they cannot participate in the Indian National Congress as a movement. Non-Hinḍūs take clauses 4, 5 and 7."

On the 21st another meeting was held of all who were working for education, or social or political reform. Various matters were discussed, and the members agreed to do everything possible in their respective neighbourhoods to unify the various bodies engaged in progressive work; to establish Libraries for books about the four departments of the forward movement; to form translation committees for the publication of leaflets and pamphlets for propaganda purposes. The co-operative movement was recognised as one of vital importance in the department of Social Reform.

Mrs. Annie Besant's carefully planned and sequential work of the last twenty years seems to be issuing in her carrying with her the bulk of the Theosophical Society—while guarding it from committing itself *as a whole* to any special opinions or activities—along the line of National Service to India, just as in England she is leading the way along a similar path, ventilating plans for profound social reorganisation, with love instead of hatred as an inspiration. She aims at the ever-closer union of the British and Indian races by mutual understanding and mutual respect. The present bold step has been led up to very gradually and quietly, and its effect on Indian public life will be watched with interest.

To this was added a second leaflet:

Some earnest workers for Social and Religious Reform have determined to make a resolute effort to serve India by bringing about the changes necessary to enable her to take her equal place among the Self-Governing Nations which owe allegiance to the British Crown. They are prepared to sacrifice themselves for this purpose, and to face the difficulties in the way of all who are ahead of their time, allying themselves with all who are working for the same end. With this object in view they have taken the following promise:

(Promise as before)

It is earnestly hoped that many religious Hindūs will join this band of workers, in order that they may preserve to India the ancient and priceless religion of Hindūism, now threatened with decay by its practical separation from the Movement of

Progress in India. The splendid heritage of spirituality and philosophy transmitted from the past, is in danger of being identified with a narrow and unprogressive orthodoxy; the life of a religion is shown by its power to adapt itself to new conditions, and while its roots are deeply struck into the past, its branches must spread far and wide, and shelter all progressive movements into which the life of the Nation is flowing. Zoroastrianism, Buḍḍhism, Islâm, are moving forwards towards a future in which all shall dwell together in civic amity, and shall co-operate for the common good. Hinḍûism, the oldest and the most widely spread faith in India, must take her place with the sister faiths, and must no longer stand apart in social isolation. Let her cast away the unessentials, and cling only to the essentials—the Immanence of God and the Solidarity of Man. All gracious customs and elevating traditions may be followed by her children, but not imposed on the unwilling, nor used as barriers to prevent social union. So shall she become a unifier instead of a divider, and again assert her glory as the most liberal of religions, the model of an active spirituality which inspires intellectual vigour, moral purity, and national prosperity.

In October and November, 1913, a series of eight lectures was delivered, each presided over by a well-known Indian gentleman, publicly connected with the subject of the lecture. They formed the public beginning of the new campaign. They aroused very great interest in Madras, and were on the following subjects:

Foreign Travel: Chairman—Dr. S. Subramania Iyer, late Acting Chief Justice of the Madras High Court.

Child-Marriage and Its Results: Chairman—The Hon. Dewān Bahāḍūr T. Sadāsiva Iyer, M.L., Acting Judge of the Madras High Court.

Our Duty to the Depressed Classes: Chairman—The Hon. Justice B. Tyabji.

Indian Industries as Related to Self-Government: Chairman—Dewān Bahāḍūr. M. Adi Narayaṇa Iyah.

Appendix to the above Lecture.

1. Exports.
2. Weaving.
3. Political Effects.
4. Moral Effects.

Mass Education: Chairman—The Hon. Justice Miller.

The Education of Indian Girls: Chairman—The Hon. Mr. P. S. Sivaswāmi Aiyer, C.I. E., C.S.I., Indian Member of the Executive Council, Madras.

The Colour Bar in England, the Colonies, and India: Chairman—The Hon. Mr. Kesava Pillai.

The Passing of the Caste System: Chairman—Dewān Bahāḍūr L. A. Govinḍarāghava Iyer.

The lectures were published as a book, which has had a very large circulation, under the title, *Wake Up, India.* The preface explained its genesis, and concluded with the significant words: "May the Guardian of India bless this effort, inspired by Him."

Those who care to read those lectures will see how the idea of a Self-Governing India underlay the changes proposed. In recommending foreign travel: I asked:

What are you looking for in the future, friends? always to remain as you are, largely aliens in your own country? or are you thinking of the time to which the late reforms are pointing, that gradually you will rise step by step, that gradually you will exercise real authority in your own land, nay, that after a time there will not only be a Parliament of India in which Indians will sit, but an Imperial Council gathered round the person of the King, in which Self-Governing India will have her representatives, as much as any other constituent part of this vast world-wide Empire. You know that my belief is that England and India are necessary the one to the other, and that the worst injury that any one can do to either is to tear these two lands apart. But union in the future will have to go on the lines of mutual respect, of liberty, of recognition of the place of Indians in India . . . there shall be one great Central Council, wherein the whole of the great Empire shall be represented. For many long years I have believed that this was coming, but I see now that it has unexpectedly come within the range of practical politics . . . I hold it up to you as an ideal to be kept before the eyes of educated India: that you will have the village Pañchāyaṭ; that you will then have the District Council, or the Municipal body; that you will have your Provincial bodies; that you will have your National body, representing India as a whole —not an unauthoritative Congress but a Parliament of India, where her people's will can be carried out in the future; then, crowning the whole, with all these Parliaments in all the many States that own our King-Emperor—whom may God long preserve —a Council of the wisest of every Nation gathered round him, a Council of the noblest of every people, a Council marked out by the character, the honour, the learning of its members; and India shall send her sons, as Canada and Australia and New Zealand and South Africa shall send theirs—the great Council of the Empire, ruling the whole under George V as King. That is what is coming.

In speaking on Industries, I said that my mind was set "on the building up of India into a mighty Self-Governing Community"; that the old system of government in India, more than any other, showed "a genius for Self-Government in the people; it shows that the Indian, as it were by nature, is capable of guiding, of shaping, of controlling his own affairs". That "competent Self-Government, effective Self-Government, can only be carried on over an area where the people who compose the governing body understand the questions with which they have to deal." I submitted that "the ancient system prevalent here dealt with things in a much more practical way, a way which made Self-Government at once effective, competent and real". If the future is to be built on the past, then we must have the Village Councils, the "grouped villages" Councils, and so on in extending areas to the District and Provincial Councils or local Parliaments, and above them the National Parliament, which would send representatives to the Imperial Council. None would be without a share in governing, but his power would be limited to the area over which his knowledge extended, and "there would be no barrier anywhere to the rising of the competent". There would be Individual Politics, or Civics, the training of the good citizen; Municipal Politics, including the grades of Councils from the Village to the Province; National Politics, the concerns of the Nation, dealt with in the National Parliament; Imperial Politics, dealing with the Empire and with international questions in the Imperial Council. I then dealt with agriculture, utilising Japanese experiments, village crafts and guilds, linking them with the Local Councils, showing how India might have "a happy, contented, agricultural and industrial population, which at present exists in no country in the world". I pointed out also how Co-operative

Societies would work in, helping home industries, cottage industries, embroidery and the "spinning of thread, which again is a woman's industry," while the men might weave. Details on weaving and other matters were given in the appendices—proposals worked out, and how they were connected with Self-Government, not mere rhapsodies on the charka and khaddar, as nine years later.

If I am to forecast the "Future of Indian Politics," I must make it clear that I believe that the destinies of Nations are planned by the Occult Hierarchy which rules the world, and are not merely the struggles, defeats, and victories, directed by Rulers, Generals, Admirals, Judges, Statesmen, and Parliaments, the actors on the stage of the World Drama. I believe that men and women, by the countless choices between the selfish and the unselfish, between personal gain and self-sacrificing service, in their preceding lives, fit themselves to play the respective leading parts of hero and villain, the smaller parts of subsidiary actors and nondescript supers in any special Act of the World Play, and I acknowledge that a Nation, a collective Will, may accept or reject an opportunity offered to it at some particular epoch, and that individuals are re-incarnated into Nations to play the parts demanded by the Great Plan, or World Drama, as when the spectator is surprised to see an army "of lions commanded by asses," in some tragedy in a Nation's life. With infinite skill, the passions and desires of men, whether good or evil, are utilised to subserve the working out of the divine purpose of evolution, that men may rise higher and higher in the Universe which lives in its perfection in the Heart of God, and is gradually worked out in the evolution of Man. "Thou makest the wrath of man to praise Thee!" sang an ancient Seer, overwhelmed with a glimpse of the Power, Wisdom and Beauty of the majestic Work.

The next step towards India's splendid destiny—hers if she rises to it during the present time of her opportunity—was to find a leader for the movement embodying the fourfold Ideal. Would the Congress take up the suggestion made in clause 7 of the promise of the Brothers of Service, and be that leader, as it seemed to me was its right? I therefore wrote to Sir Pherozeshah Mehta and Mr. Dadabhai Naoroji, to ask whether the National Congress would put itself at the head, and take the direction, of a National movement embodying religious, educational and social, as well as political, reforms. It seemed to me that the National Congress could not ultimately succeed, unless its programme included the four aspects of National Life, but I felt that those who had created and led the Congress were those who had the right to decide its action, and that I had no right beyond making the suggestion. Sir Pherozeshah wrote to me that the question had arisen very early in the life of the Congress, and that it had been decided that opinions varied so much on religious, educational and social questions, that it was thought to be best that those who agreed on the broad lines of Political Reform should not mar their unity by introducing other matters. He wrote very kindly and invited me to talk things over with him, and I gladly assented, but his illness prevented the meeting. Mr. Dadabhai Naoroji agreed with him as to keeping the political movement separate. I therefore started a weekly newspaper, *The Commonweal*, on January 2, 1914, to embody the fourfold Ideal, and an article with the caption, "Our Policy" sets it forth. Declaring that a free platform should be kept by the journal for the thoughtful discussion of the four classes of subjects, it gave its editorial policy:

> The editorial policy regards the four great functions of human life—belonging to the Spirit, the Mind, the Emotions and the Body—as being different expressions of One Life, and as therefore closely inter-related. They form the four great departments of National Reform in every country, and any antagonism between them, nay, any mutual coldness or indifference, throws the whole Body Politic out of health.
>
> In India, this isolation is peculiarly mischievous, because, as Mr. A. O. Hume pointed out in 1885: "The earnest and unselfish labourers for progress in this country constitute but an infinitesimal fraction of the population, a fraction that becomes absolutely inappreciable if further subdivided." We stand, then, for Union among all workers in the National Cause, and ask only to be allowed to serve it in any of the four great departments.

In *Religion*, it stood for individual liberty, mutual respect, regarding all religions as ways to God, and recognising the religious consciousness, not any outer authority, as the Inner Ruler of each. It asked that all should be protected in their liberty, and that none should be privileged. In *Education*, it pleaded for flexibility, fewer examinations, for encouragement of initiative in teachers and pupils, inclusion of physical, moral and religious culture, the lowering of fees, the encouragement of the vernaculars and classical languages of India, more schools and colleges, more technical and artistic instruction, education of girls and of the masses, and generally for universal education on National lines, "with an open path from primary schools through higher schools to the Universities". In *Social Reform*, it advocated foreign travel, co-operation, uplift of the submerged classes, with abolition of child-marriage, seclusion of women, colour bar and the caste system. I add the full statement of the Political Reform desired, because it outlines what we meant by Self-Government and the way to it and the spirit in which it was framed, a spirit of union, love, and co-operation, not of disunion, hatred and non-co-operation. It indicates our political aim, the Free Future of India, that which we laboured for in the Home Rule League, the Congress-League Scheme, the Montagu-Chelmsford Reforms, the working of Reforms, and in the later opposition to the Non-Co-Operation movement, led by Mr. Gandhi. It runs:

In Political Reform we aim at the building up of complete Self-Government from Village Councils, through District and Municipal Boards and Provincial Legislative Assemblies, to a National Parliament, equal in its powers to the legislative bodies of the Self-Governing Colonies, by whatever name these may be called; also at the direct representation of India in the Imperial Parliament, when that body shall contain representatives of the Self-Governing States of the Empire. All measures that tend in this direction we shall support, and all that retard it we shall oppose. We recognise the National Congress and the non-official members of representative bodies as voicing the will of India. We claim an open path for Indians to every post in their native land, as promised by the Proclamation of 1858, and the abolition of every law that places them in a position inferior to that enjoyed by the English. We ask that capacity and high character shall determine all appointments to office, and that colour and religion shall be entirely disregarded as qualifications.

One thing that lies very near to our heart is to draw Great Britain and India nearer to each other, by making known in Great Britain something of Indian movements, and of the men who will influence from here the destinies of the Empire.

In 1914, I went to England, and there tried, but failed, to form a little party in the House of Commons to promote Indian interests. It failed because the Home Rule question in Ireland was before the House, and its supporters feared to embarrass Mr. Asquith, the then Premier, by starting a party advocating Home Rule for India. However, I lectured for India, and in the Great Queen's Hall, Earl Brassey in the Chair, I explained her grievances and her needs, and finally declared that "The price of India's loyalty is India's Freedom." Mr. Jinnah and Lālā Lājpaṭ Rai supported me, and the meeting was a great success.

On my return to India, I started a daily newspaper to advocate the same policy as that of *The Commonweal*, purchasing *The Madras Standard.* The first number was issued on July 14, 1914, and it was soon renamed *New India.* It sounded out the Self-Government note of 1906 and urged that instead of asking for Reforms piecemeal, we should bend our energies to win Self-Government, Home Rule, and make the reforms for ourselves. In an article on July 23, on "National Education," I pleaded that the coming Hindū University should be a "National," not a "Government" University, with power to make its own curriculum, and controlled by Indians. (Both points were gained.) In that article occurs the following:

> Let an Englishman imagine what Eton and Harrow, Oxford and Cambridge would be, if they were held and administered by Germans; would they any longer be nurseries of English heroism, of English patriotism? Would English boys brought

up on German history, or biographies of German heroes, on the lives of Blucher and Bismarck, become the Englishmen that carry the English flag to every quarter of the globe? Let them then realise how Indians feel, who have behind them a civilisation of thousands of years, and whose sons are now brought up on lives which make them regard their forefathers—who produced the Upaniṣhaṭs, the *Mahābhāraṭa*, the dramas of Kāliḍāsa, the commentaries of Shaṅkarāchārya, Rāmānuja and Māḍhva, the devotion of Tukàràm, Kabir and Guru Nānak, the valour of Pratāp Singh, the statesmanship of Akbar—as a crowd of superstitious dreamers and impracticable visionaries, while they are taught to look to Nelson and Wellington as heroes, and to regard important Indian history as beginning with Clive and Warren Hastings. We do not blame the Government; how should Englishmen understand the, to them, foreign splendours of an ancient eastern land? They have given us of their best, and never will India forget that we owe to them the uplifting before Indian eyes of the ideals of Liberty and Self-Government, the inspiration of ordered Freedom, of National self-consciousness; we owe to them the training of the present generation of vakils, doctors, great merchants, who founded and have carried on the National Congress, who formed Indian public opinion, the "educated minority," regarded by *The Times* with a hatred born of fear, and by India as its present glory, and its future hope.

But we cannot sacrifice Indian Nationality on the altar of our gratitude to our English rulers. And that gratitude is best shown by carrying into practice what they have taught us as to the value of patriotism and public spirit, as exemplified in themselves, offering them the highest compliment of imitation. Moreover we know that we still need their help in this transition period, during which an ancient civilisation is transforming itself into a modern one; and that help will be most gratefully welcomed if the condition of its acceptance be not the confession of National inferiority. England and India will be most closely bound together if they work hand in hand and heart with heart, to make India a Self-Governing community in the great Federated Empire, whose majestic outlines are dimly seen in the sky of the future.

The War did not break out until the August of that year, and when I left England for Home in June, there was no shadow to be seen of the rapidly approaching storm. It cannot, then, be pretended, with any truth or honesty, that India made her first move towards Self-Government as a result of the War, and took advantage of the danger and difficulties into which Britain was plunged.

On the contrary, when War broke out, India's first impulse, first movement, was to spring to the side of Britain, to help her, to fight beside her, to live or die with her. To India, Germany embodied Autocracy, and Britain Liberty. She thrilled to the words of Asquith and Lloyd George. She was aflame with enthusiastic pride and love. The Madras Bar volunteered with eagerness, and the first chill came with the rejection of their warm-hearted enthusiasm. The offer of their manhood refused, they gave their money, and the first Hospital Ship was that of Madras. I embodied in my Editorial Notes in *The Theosophist* for November, 1914, the feelings which throbbed in all our hearts in those first months of War, and I put it on record here, that I may bear witness for those who worked politically in India from 1914 to 1919 for the ideals for which our men, Indians and English alike, were fighting in the trenches of north-eastern

France and Flanders, in Gallipoli, in Mesopotamia, in Palestine, in East Africa, that they fought here against the autocracy which India and Britain were destroying in Europe, with the words of English leaders on their lips, and the love of English Freedom in their hearts. The war for Liberty abroad fired us to win Liberty at Home, that our soldiers might return to an India growing into Freedom. The wave of passion for Liberty that swept over the world, and at last drove America into the War, with Wilson's ringing words, could not leave India untouched, but set her heart a-throbbing. And so I wrote :

All the world over is the tumult of War; the lurid light of devastated homes blazes out from the burning towns of Belgium; the relics of past ages in Louvain and Rheims and Dinant have been hammered into pieces by the new hammer of Thor; hundreds of thousands of men, killed or wounded, strew the fields that should have been yellowing for the sickle; all the fair peaceful industries of common life are whelmed in one red ruin.

And for what is all this pain, this agony of wrenched muscles and shattered limbs, this blasting of bright young lives, this destruction of glowing hopes? In the pictures of the killed that appear in the illustrated papers, there are so many faces glad with the sunshine of life, bright faces of young manhood, dawning into virility, faces that mothers must have loved so dearly, must have kissed so passionately as they sent them forth. As one looks at them, one sees them trampled into crimson mud, shattered by bursting shell, riven by cut of sabre, and is glad that the earth should hide the horror of what was once so fair. Clear eyes, looking out so brightly upon joyous life, that have gazed unflinchingly into the eyes of death. Lips, still showing the gracious curves of youth, that hardened in the battle-crash, to relax again only in the peace of death.

And all for what? For what the broken hearts in all the homes in which these gallant lads were light and joy? For what the anguish of the widows of these other men, beyond the first flush of youth, who left behind them their earth's treasure, with the children who shall watch for their father's coming, useless watching, for homeward he will never come again? For what the myriads of darkened homes, whose breadwinners, husbands and sons, fathers and lovers, find no record in the pictured pages, though dear to the hearts that love them as are the noble and wealthy who thereon have their place? For what the world's great anguish, mourning over her slaughtered sons? For what?

There have been wars begun for transient objects, for the conquest of a piece of land, for the weakening of a rival, for the gaining of added power, begun because of ambition, of greed, of jealousy, of insult. In such wars, lives are flung away for trifles, though the men who suffer in them, or who die, win out of their own anguish added strength and beauty of character, full reward for the pain endured; for they return with the spoils of victory into new avenues of ascending life, and with them it is very well. Such wars are evil in their origin, however much the divine alchemy may transmute the base into fine gold.

But this War is none of these. In this War mighty Principles are battling for the mastery. Ideals are locked in deadly combat. The direction of the march of our present civilisation, upwards or downwards, depends on the issue of the struggle. Two Ideals of World-Empire are balanced on the scales of the future. That is what raises this War above all others known in the brief history of the West; it is the latest of the pivots on which, in successive ages, the immediate future of the world has turned. To die, battling for the Right, is the gladdest fate that can befall the youth in the joy of his dawning manhood, the man in the pride of his strength, the elder in the wisdom of his maturity, aye, and the aged in the rich splendour of his whitened head. To be wounded in this War is to be enrolled in the ranks of Humanity's Warriors, to have felt the stroke of the sacrificial knife, to bear in the mortal body the glorious scars of an immortal struggle.

Of the two possible World-Empires, that of Great Britain and that of Germany, one is already far advanced in the making and shows its quality, with Dominions and Colonies, with India at its side. The other is but in embryo, but can be judged by its theories, with the small examples available as to the fashion of their outworking in the few Colonies that it is founding, the outlining of the unborn embryo.

The first embodies—though as yet but partially realised—the Ideal of Freedom; of ever-increasing Self-Government; of Peoples rising into power and self-development along their own lines; of a Supreme Government "broad-based upon the People's Will"; of fair and just treatment of undeveloped races, aiding not enslaving them; it embodies the embryo of the splendid Democracy of the Future; of the New Civilisation, co-operative, peaceful, progressive, artistic, just, and free—a Brotherhood of Nations, whether the Nations be inside or outside the World-Empire. This is the Ideal; and that Great Britain has set her feet in the path which leads to it is proved, not only by her past interior history with its struggles towards Liberty, but also by her granting of autonomy to her Colonies, her formation of the beginnings of Self-Government in India, her constantly improving attitude towards the undeveloped races—as in using the Salvation Army to civilise the criminal tribes in India—all promising advances towards the Ideal. Moreover, she has ever sheltered the oppressed exiles, flying to her shores for refuge against their tyrants—the names of Kossuth, Mazzini, Kropotkin, shine out gloriously as witnesses in her favour; she has fought against the slave-trade and wellnigh abolished it. And at the present moment she is fighting in defence of keeping faith with those too small to exact it; in defence of Treaty obligations and the sanctity of a Nation's pledged word; in defence of National Honour, of Justice to the weak, of that Law, obedience to which by the strong States is the only guarantee of future Peace, the only safeguard of Society against the tyranny of brute Strength. For all this England is fighting, when she might have stood aside, selfish and at ease, watching her neighbours tearing each other into pieces, waiting until their exhaustion made it possible for her to impose her will. Instead of thus remaining, she has sprung forward, knight-errant of Liberty, servant of Duty. With possible danger of Civil War behind her, with supposed possible revolt in South Africa and India, with shameful bribes offered for her standing aside, she spurned all lower reasonings, and springing to her feet, sent out a lion's roar of defiance to the breakers of treaties, uttered a ringing shout for help to her peoples, flung her little army to the front—a veritable David against Goliath—to gain time, time, that the hosts might gather, to hold the enemy back at all costs, let die who might of her children; called for men to her standard, men from the nobles, from the professions, from the trades, men from the plough, from the forge, from the mine, from the furnace; and this not for gain—she has naught to gain from the War—but because she loved Liberty, Honour, Justice, Law, better than life or treasure, that she counted glorious Death a thousandfold more desirable than shameful existence bought by cowardly ease. For this, the Nations bless her; for this, her dying Sons adore her; for this, History shall applaud her; for this, shall the World-Empire be hers with the consent of all Free Peoples, and she shall be the Protector, not the Tyrant, of Humanity.

The second claimant of World-Empire embodies the Ideal of Autocracy founded on Force. The candidate proclaims himself the War Lord, and in his realm no Master save himself; he declares to his army, as he flings his sword into the scale of War:

> Remember that the German people are the chosen of God. On me, on me, as German Emperor, the Spirit of God has descended. I am His weapon, His sword, and His Vicegerent. Woe to the disobedient. Death to cowards and unbelievers.

The thinkers, the teachers of his people, have formulated the theory of the World-Empire; it recognises no law in dealing with States save that of Strength, no arbitrament save War. Its own self-interest is declared to be its only motive; its morality is based on the increase of the power of its Empire; the weak must have no rights; the conquered Nations must be "left only eyes to weep with"; woe to the conquered! woe to the weak! woe to the helpless! all religions save the Religion of Force are superstitious, their morality is outgrown. Murder, robbery, arson—all are permissible, nay, praiseworthy in invading hosts. Mercy is contemptible. Chivalry is an anachronism. Compassion is feebleness. Art and Literature have no sanctity. The women, the children, the aged—they are all weak; why should not strong men use them as they will? All undeveloped races are the prey of the "civilised". And we are not left without signs of the application of the theory. Herr Schlettwein instructs the German Reichstag on the "Principles of Colonisation":

> The Hereros must be compelled to work, and to work without compensation and in return for their food only. Forced labour for years is only a just punishment, and at the same time it is the best method of training them. The feelings of Christianity and philanthropy, with which the missionaries work, must for the present be repudiated with all energy.

General von Trotha, tired even of enslaving them, proclaims:

> The Herero people must now leave the land. If it refuses I shall compel it with the gun. Within the German frontier every Herero, with or without weapon, with or without cattle, will be shot. I shall take charge of no more women and children, but shall drive them back to their people or let them be shot at.

The proclamation was carried out; thousands were shot; thousands were "driven into a waterless desert where they perished of hunger and thirst". On this sample, we refuse the goods offered. Moreover, we have seen the Empire at work, carrying out in Belgium its theories of murder, rape, and loot. The "chosen people of the (German) God" stink in the nostrils of Europe. This embryo-Empire of the bottomless pit, conceived of Hatred and shaped in the womb of Ambition, must never come to the birth. It is the New Barbarism; it is the antithesis of all that is noble, compassionate, and humane. Humanity knows the ways of Goths, Vandals and Huns, the Berserker rage of the Vikings; it refuses to bow down before the Idol of Force, the Negation of Law, of Freedom, of Justice and of Peace. They that make the sword the arbitrament shall perish by the sword. The War Germany has provoked, as her road to Empire, shall crush her militarism, free her people, and usher in the reign of Peace.

Because these things are so, because the fate of the next Age of the World turns now on the choice made by the Nations, I call on all who are pledged to Universal Brotherhood, all Theosophists the world over, to stand for Right against Might, Law against Force, Freedom against Slavery, Brotherhood against Tyranny.

Surely that was not a spirit of taking advantage of the War to press a new claim for Dominion status.

CHAPTER II

A NEW DEPARTURE

AT the Twenty-ninth National Congress in Madras in December, 1914, a new departure was taken. (For those who may be puzzled, on referring to the Congress Reports, by finding this Congress called the Twenty-ninth, instead of the Thirtieth, I may explain that the Congress broken up at Surat in 1907 was the Twenty-third. It was adjourned, not dissolved, and met again at Madras, in 1908, with the same President, the Hon. Mr. Rāsh Bihāri Ghose, as still the Twenty-third Congress. Thenceforward the number of the Congress is one less than it should be according to the years since 1885.)

Before the Congress of 1914 met, a fateful decision had been taken, which re-united the

Indian political party, split in two at Surat in 1907, and thereafter known as "Extremists" and "Congressmen". The union completed at Lucknow, in 1916, was again threatened in 1918, and broken definitely in 1919 over the Reform Act of that year. On that occasion, however, the Congress went with the "Extremists," and the "Moderates" and "National Home Rulers" took no further part in it, the Special Congress of 1920, at Calcutta, adopting Mr. Gandhi's method of Non-Co-Operation, and the Annual Congress at Nāgpūr, 1920, changing its creed and constitution. That, however, is only a hasty glance forward. We must return to 1914.

Staying with Mr. Gokhale in the Servants of India Society's home in Poona, in the autumn of 1914, he asked me to go to Mr. Tilak, his old enemy, and see if a *via media* could not be found for joining into one body all who desired India's freedom, so that the great split made at Surat might be healed. He showed me the outline of Reforms that he had drawn up, and suggested that Mr. Tilak and his powerful party might re-enter the Congress, and a United India might work for Self-Government within the Empire on "Colonial lines," as the creed of the Congress laid down. I went and saw Mr. Tilak—who had been a member of the Theosophical Society in the early days, as were so many of the original Congressmen—and we had some conversations. Ultimately, we came to a preliminary agreement; Mr. Tilak came to see Mr. Gokhale, and it was agreed that a proposal, drawn up by Mr. Gokhale, should be put before the coming Congress, to open the way for the return into the Congress of the "Extremists," as they were then called. Unhappily, a cruel accusation was flung at Mr. Gokhale, touching his honour, just before the Congress, and he sent a message to me, bidding me not bring forward his proposal. I, of course dropped it, but having promised to place before the Committee a suggestion that certain modifications should be made in the rule for election of delegates, and there being no time to communicate with Mr. Gokhale, I made, but did not carry, that proposal, entirely on my own account. He was angry with me for the moment, but when I pointed out that, with his consent, I had pledged myself to do so, he, ever just, approved, and said that, some months later, his proposal might be made, but he could not move then. Alas! he passed away in the February of 1915—for those who like coincidences, I may note that he left us on February 19th, the day on which occurred, in 1861, the Liberation of the Russian serfs, a good day for one who was one of the Liberators of India. Still, in the Congress of 1915, the necessary change was made, and the "Tilak party" rejoined the Congress in 1916, at Lucknow.

of the Arms Act were asked for, so that it should "apply equally to all persons residing in or visiting India," and the pride of the Nation in its troops in the firing-line was warmly expressed. In relation to Indians abroad, the suggestion of the Viceroy (Lord Hardinge) was approved that Reciprocity should be the rule between India and the Colonies, and it remarked that

> any policy of Reciprocity to be effective and acceptable to the people of India must proceed on the basis that the Government of India should possess and exercise the same power of dealing with the Colonies as they possess and exercise with regard to India.

This assertion of the equality of India with the Self-Governing Colonies marks the sense of the Congress that the Crown, in calling for the equality of India with those Colonies in duty to, and in suffering and sacrifice for, the Empire, had implicitly and *de facto* acknowledged her equality with them in the Empire, and in Resolution X it asked that that equality might also be recognised *de jure*. As a matter of fact, there was no equality of sacrifice in the Colonies and India, for India had long, at a huge and ever-increasing cost, maintained *on a War footing* an Army far beyond her needs, and it was this which enabled Lord Hardinge to fling across the seas into France an Army ready to take the field, right athwart the path to Paris between the advancing hosts of Germany and the splendid, but worn out, "contemptible little Army" of Britain; to falsify the boast of the Kaiser that he would "dine in Paris in a fortnight"; to save Britain in the hour of her bitter need. The Germans would have won while the Colonies were preparing and Britain was training their raw levies after they landed; and the frantic enthusiasm with which Parliament welcomed the arrival of the Indians, at that critical moment, showed its sense of the imminence of

Britain's peril, and of the greatness of the service rendered to the Empire by India. Britain would doubtless have won in the end, but, with the Germans in Paris, she would probably have suffered the horrors of invasion.

As the enthusiasm faded with the passing of the immediate peril, and troops poured in in from the Colonies, while few of that first Army remained alive, I will put on record here the evidence of General Sir James Willcocks, K.C.B., G.C.M.G., K.C.S.I., D.S.O., LL.D., in his invaluable book *With the Indians in France*, published in 1920. It is dedicated:

TO MY BRAVE COMRADES
OF ALL RANKS OF THE INDIAN ARMY
I DEDICATE THIS BOOK, WHICH IS AN
EARNEST ENDEAVOUR TO RECORD THEIR
LOYALTY AND UNPERISHABLE VALOUR
ON THE BATTLE-FIELDS OF
FRANCE AND BELGIUM

Sir James Willcocks claims, in his Introduction that "few, if any, have a better knowledge of the brave Indian soldiers and the deeds they performed than I have". He remarks that they could not have done what they did "without the help and example of their illustrious comrades of the Scotch, Irish and English battalions which formed part of each brigade, or of the splendid Territorial units which later joined us, and the superb British artillery which paved the way for all our efforts. But," he said only too truly, "of these History will assuredly furnish a brilliant account. It is not always so of Indian troops . . . The rank and file will furnish no writers to thrill the generations to come; they will just pass with the great masses of India, content that they have done their duty and been faithful to their salt." I remember how one of the Anzacs said, after returning to Australia: "An Indian was a good pal to have beside you in the trenches." He concludes the Introduction by saying that it is due to India that the facts should be told:

> The day is past when that great portion of our Empire could be kept in comparative darkness; the light is dawning, and the Great War has opened to her an opportunity which she never had before. Her sons have shared the glory of the Empire. From the boggy fields and trenches of Flanders and the desert sands of Egypt; from the immortal heights of Gallipoli; from the burning plains of Mesopotamia and the impenetrable jungles of East Africa, comes up with one voice, from the thousands who fought and bled for England:
>
> India has taken a new birth;
> The heavens above, the sea, the earth
> Have changed for aye, the darkness dies,
> Light has illumined all men's eyes,
> Since Armageddon's day.

Sir James commanded for a year an Indian Army Corps, "for the first time in history to be employed in Europe". He remarks that "the Army of India was little understood in Great Britain, where newspaper writers thought that it was composed of Sikhs and Gurkhas," where a Sikh squadron was described as "fierce turbaned Muslims on fiery Arab steeds," and the artillery "composed of the finest British batteries," "superbly horsed," was reported by one paper as consisting of "mountain guns borne on Abyssinian mules". But the gem was from a foreign paper, announcing the arrival of the first Army Corps at Marseille:

> This Corps has been raised and equipped entirely at the expense of three great Indian Princes, who are now occupying the finest hotel in Marseille. Their names are Prince Sikya (evidently a corruption of Sikh); Prince Gorok (Gurkhas); and Prince Balukin (meant for Baluchis).

Sir James mentions the special difficulties of the Indians, their old rifles replaced with fresh ones at Marseille, new ammunition, the use of hand-grenades and trench mortars, and other shortages of things, "essential to a force suddenly dumped down from railhead into the trenches". He says:

> I have no desire unnecessarily to string out the manifest disadvantages the Indian Corps laboured

under, but I have heard too much the criticisms of our Indian troops by soldiers and civilians, who are without the faintest knowledge of what they talk about, and it is only right that the truth should be known. There is a growing body of Indians who have every desire but no means of ascertaining the facts, and if this book can be of any use in helping to explain to my numberless friends and acquaintances in India the splendid deeds of their brethren who fought and bled on the sodden plains of Flanders, under handicaps which must have been seen and felt to be understood, I shall be more than rewarded. Moreover, as commander of those troops during a year of war I had opportunities of knowing many details unknown to others, and now that the war is over I am free to write the truth which for years has been of necessity suppressed.

Whatever may have been the shortcomings of the Indian army, it possessed one asset which never stood it in better stead than in France; its British officers, although far too small in number, were the salt of the earth. As leaders of men, comrades and friends of their Indian officers, sepoys, and sowars, as loyal and brave gentlemen, they could not be surpassed. I always believed in them, but in France my belief was heightened to profound admiration, and as death took its heavy toll day by day, I knew that by no means could they be replaced; for the great essential was that they should know their men and their language, and this became impossible as India sent more and more troops to the various theatres of war.

Next to the British were the Indian officers, most of them men who had earned their commissions by brave and loyal service, of fighting stock, with martial traditions, ready to give their lives for their King-Emperor, proud of their profession of arms; they formed the essential link between the British officers and men. In ordinary circumstances in the Field they were well fitted to fill temporarily the place of their lost British leaders.

Despite this, he says:

One of my chief difficulties at the beginning of this war was to make it understood that the Indians cannot be treated as pure machines, and that they possess national characteristics as varied as those between Scandinavians and Italians. I own that Sir John French and his Staff generally made every allowance for these facts, but there were others who made none; an Army Corps (no matter its fighting strength in numbers) was an Army Corps and nothing else. An Army Corps was supposed to be able to occupy so many thousand yards of trenches, and the orders were issued by this routine rule.

It might be said the Indian Corps was sent as a Corps, and times were too pressing to go into such details; this is perhaps true, and we all recognised it at the beginning of the Flanders fighting; but as time went on and the German attack was beaten off, I saw plainly that you cannot expect a ship to keep up full steam when the engineers and stokers are lying shattered in the hold. And yet those brave men not only filled a big gap in our battered line, but, helped and encouraged by their comrades of the British battalions of the Indian Corps, held it against incessant attack. Minenwerfers, hand grenades, and high explosives tore through them and flattened out their trenches; blood flowed freely; but as often as they were driven back from their defences they managed to return to them again. India has reason to be proud of her sons, and their children may well tell with pride of the deeds of their fathers.

He shows a clear appreciation of Indian feeling when he says of Indian officers:

They should be given rank corresponding to their British comrades, and precedence equal to, if not above, their civilian confrères. To the ordinary observer like myself, at Darbars and public gatherings, it was plain that they never received their proper share of Izzat (honour). No doubt I shall be told this was all thought out and arranged by the Government, but I speak from practical experience, not from the edicts of Simla and Delhi. The Indian officer was not treated with the respect which was his due, and which he has earned in arduous service on many fields of war. It was a feeling very strongly held by them and must be set right. Izzat is a thing little understood by any but Indians, but it is a great driving force; it raises men in the estimation of their fellows, whilst the loss of it debases them.

In judging the effect of the War on India's outlook, we must take account of the fact that the few survivors, who returned from the early days of the War to their villages, brought with them the memories of their comrades in the trenches, the memories of the white troops they fought against, the memories of the gallant deeds performed by Indian soldiers, and of the honour paid to them in France and England. Thus the villagers came into touch with a larger life, a wider outlook, a knowledge of free countries, and of the honours won by Indians in the fields, where they fought beside and against the finest white soldiers in the world. I do not think that the share of the War in arousing National pride has been fitly recognised, nor the result of coming back from free countries, where they had fought for freedom and left their dead behind, into a country where, despite all they had suffered, they found themselves still under the "intolerable degradation" of the yoke of a foreign Nation.

To return to the Congress of 1914. The Resolution ran:

> X. *Resolved*—That in view of the profound and avowed loyalty that the people of India have manifested in the present crisis, this Congress appeals to the Government to deepen and perpetuate it, and make it an enduring and valuable asset of the Empire, by removing all invidious distinctions here and abroad, between His Majesty's Indian and other subjects, by redeeming the pledges of Provincial Autonomy contained in the Despatch of the 25th August, 1911, and by taking such measures as may be necessary for the recognition of India as a component part of a federated Empire, in the full and the free enjoyment of the rights belonging to that status.

Thus was the note struck. The Resolution was moved by the well-known patriot, Mr. Surendranath Bannerji, in a well-reasoned speech, basing India's claim on the Proclamation of 1858 and the Despatch of August 25, 1911, and declaring in favour of "a number of administrations, autonomous in all provincial affairs, with the Government of India above them, and possessing powers to interfere in case of mis-government". He asked the audience to formulate a scheme and press it on the British public. In supporting it, I urged on the younger men, "who will be part of the Self-Governing Nation," to practise the science and art of Government in local bodies, and asked Congress to form a definite scheme of Self-Government to present to England after the War.

After a year of vigorous propaganda the Congress of 1915 ordered its Committees to prepare such a scheme.

CHAPTER III

THE GREAT AGITATION

AND very vigorous that propaganda was, all the circumstances of the time co-operating to increase its intensity. In the propaganda, *New India* and *The Commonweal* led the way, with stirring articles and outspoken directness, new in Indian politics. It was an English political agitation, carried on with unbroken energy. But other means were adopted, in addition to a daily and a weekly paper. On New Year's Day, 1915, it was proposed to start a "Madras Parliament," *i.e.*, a Debating Society which observed Parliamentary forms, for it was thought that as we were aiming at Home Rule, it would be well to train ourselves in the careful study of National problems, and the methods of producing measures accurately and systematically; the reports of the debates, and the circulation of the Transactions in the form of Acts, would all serve to arouse and discipline political activity. A Committee of 17 persons formed itself early in February, 1915, and drew up rules; the Hon. Mr. Justice Sadasivier was invited to be the first Speaker and accepted the office; Ḍewān Bahāḍūr L. A. Govindarāghava Iyer, was offered the post of Leader of the House, but as he declined, it was left to the members to elect their own man (*Commonweal*, February 12, 1915, pp. 125, 126). The inaugural meeting was held on February 14, when, after the registration of members, Annie Besant was elected Prime Minister, and March 6 was fixed for the first business meeting. (*Ibid.*, February 19, p. 136.)

In *The Commonweal* of February 26 the first Ministry is announced (p. 27): *Prime*

Minister and Secretary for the Treasury, Annie Besant. *Under-Secretary* (not yet chosen). *Local Government Board*, T. Rangāchāri. *Under-Secretary*, K. C. Ḍesikāchāriar. *Education*, C. P. Rāmaswāmi Aiyar. *Under-Secretary*, C. Jinarājaḍāsa. *Industries*, Hon. Mr. B. N. Sarma. *Under-Secretary* (not yet chosen). *Commerce*, Rai Sāhab G. Soobbiah Chetty. *Under-Secretary*, C. Gopala Menon. *Co-operation*, Ḍewān Bahāḍūr M. Auḍinarāyaṇa Iyah. *Under-Secretary*, V. Venkatasubbaya. *Home Department*, Ḍewān Bahāḍūr L. A. Govinḍarāghava Iyer. *Under-Secretary*, Hon. Mr. V. S. Srinivāsa Sāsṭri. R. B. Aingar, Barr-at-Law, was Clerk of the House. The Whips, C. S. Govinḍarāja Muḍaliar and J. R. Aria. The Parliament met on March 6, and its first meeting was held under the shadow of a great loss. I had consulted Mr. Gokhale on the subject and he gave it his "enthusiastic approval," and on February 13 wired his wish that it should be helped; almost a dying wish, as he passed away on February 19. I wrote on February 26: "Needless to say I had counted on his advice as it went on, for early in 1914, he had accepted me as a fellow-worker in the political field, and I relied on his experience for counsel in any political work, and did not intend to take any step without his sanction. *New India* was placed at his disposal as soon as purchased, and he had intended to use it in preparation for the next Congress, to which, with improved health he was looking forward." Under his blessing, the Parliament did much useful work. I see names now in the Council of State, the Legislative Assembly, the Madras Legislative Council, who are working in real Parliaments and practised their 'prentice efforts in our local Parliament. The latter died in June, 1917, when three of its members were interned, and the others threw themselves into the vehement agitation that brought about the famous Declaration of August 20, 1917, and released the internees.

The Transactions bore the stirring motto:

> We bring the Light that saves,
> We bring the Morning Star;
> Freedom's good things we bring you,
> Whence all good things are.

Act I, 1915, was Compulsory Elementary Education, brought in by C. P. Rāmaswāmi Aiyar, the most brilliant member of our body, in an admirable speech; others published were the Madras Pañchāyaṭs Act, prepared by Mr. T. Raṅgāchāri, the most complete measure on the subject that I have seen and a guide for a future Act; the Commonwealth of India Act, brought in by myself, and followed by a Supplementary Act on the Indian Judicature, brought in by Mr. C. P. Rāmaswāmi Aiyar; a Religious Education Act, by Mr. C. Jinarājaḍāsa; a very full and careful Emigration Act was brought in by Mr. B. P.

Wadia, but was not published. These measures were very vigorously debated, Mr. G. S. Arundale making a most dashing leader of the Opposition.

Another series of papers of which a huge number were circulated, were the "*New India* Political Pamphlets," each of which bore the motto

> How long ere thou take station?
> How long ere thralls live free?

We, in fact, flooded the country with tracts, gave lectures, carried on, as said, a very vigorous propaganda.

During this year was also published in *The Commonweal*, *How India Wrought for Freedom*, a narrative of the Congress from 1885 to 1914, published later as a book and prefaced by a Historical Introduction, which infuriated the Anglo-Indian Press, because it was a narrative of facts, and could only be abused, not disproved.

The formation of a Home Rule League was discussed and worked for. The country caught eagerly at the idea, and in September I went to Bombay to consult Mr. Dadabhai Naoroji on the subject, and received his hearty approval. The local leaders, however, did not welcome the idea, thinking it might weaken the Congress, whereas the hope was to strengthen it. It was because the Congress showed little activity between its annual sessions that the need for a Home Rule League had arisen, to be an active propagandist body, to carry on a steady and powerful agitation for Home Rule. The words " Home Rule " were chosen as a short, popular cry, marking the fact that the struggle was not against Great Britain, but for Liberty within the Empire. So successful was the cry that by 1917 the words had become, as Mr. Gandhi said, " a manṭram in every cottage ". In a Gujerāṭi paper, India was pictured as a woman blowing a trumpet, from the mouth of which issued the English words, "Home Rule". One thing specially aimed at was a common platform on which Hindūs and Muslims could work together, instead of regularly working apart in a National Congress, to which few Musalmâns came, and an All-India Muslim League to which only Muslims were admitted.

While this many-featured and powerful educational agitation—a thoroughly healthy and constitutional one, never once disfigured by violence—was going on all over the country, the circumstances of the time were such as to force the Nation rapidly forward into a consciousness of Nationhood, and of her then place in the eyes of the world, a place so unworthy of her storied past, and of the virility of her people in the present, when stirred by a call that moved them to exertion. That call came from the War, which became more and more terrible as it swept over the lands, and India became full of pride in the prowess of her soldiers, fighting side by side with the flower of European troops, and fighting against the mightiest army in the world. India felt herself living as her children died for Freedom, and the villages which sent their men became conscious of a wider and more stirring world. The words of English statesmen, spoken to enhearten their own countrymen, rang across the seas to India. Asquith spoke of what England would feel if Germans filled her highest offices, controlled her policy, levied her taxes, made her laws; it would be inconceivable, he cried, and intolerable. India listened, and murmured to herself: "But that is exactly my condition; here, these same Englishmen think it the only conceivable and the only tolerable life for me." He spoke of the "intolerable degradation of a foreign yoke"; India whispered: "Is it so? Do Englishmen think thus? What, then, of me?"

She had accepted English rule by habit; now she was shocked into realising the position which she filled in the eyes of the world. A subject Nation. A subject race. Was that really how the white Nations looked on her? Was that why her sons were treated as coolies in the outside world? Did a foreign yoke at home mean unspeakable humiliations abroad?

Then the pride of the Aryan Motherland awoke. Had she not a civilisation dating back by millennia, beside which these white races, sprung from her womb, were but of yesterday? Had she not been rich, strong, and self-ruled, while these wandered naked in their forests, and quarrelled with each other? Had she not lived as equal with the mightiest Nations of a far-off past, when Babylon was the wonder of the world, when the streets of Nineveh were crowded, when Egypt was the teacher of wisdom, when Persia was a mighty Empire, when Greek philosophy was an offshoot of her schools, when Rome clad her haughtiest matrons in the products of her looms? Had not many a Nation invaded her, and had she not either driven them back, or assimilated them, and re-created them into Indians? Had not the gold of the world flowed into her coffers? *Yet now she was poor.* Had not great Empires, now dead, sent ambassadors to her Courts? *But now she was "a Dependency" of a little far-off Island in northern seas.* She had been asleep. She had been dreaming. But now she awakened. She opened her eyes, and looked around her. She saw her peasants, starving at home, but holding their own as soldiers abroad. The coolies, despised in England's Colonies, were cheered as heroes by Englishmen in the streets of their capital city. Yes, Asquith was right: "the intolerable degradation of a foreign yoke". If she was worthy to fight for Freedom, she was worthy to enjoy it. If she stood equal with Englishmen, Scotchmen,

Colonials, in the trenches, and her poured-out blood mingled with theirs, indistinguishably soaking into French and Flemish soil, then she should be equal with them in her own ancient land. The souls of her dead in France, in Belgium, in Gallipoli, in Palestine, in Syria, in Mesopotamia, in East Africa, cried to her to claim the Freedom for which their bodies lay scattered far from home and kin. India sprang to her feet—a Nation.

And then, because a white woman had been crying in her sleeping ears these truths about herself for more than twenty years, and was crying them aloud still in her ears awakened by the crash of War, she turned to her for a while as her natural leader, who had blown the conch for Liberty's battle in India. And she sang:

WAKE UP, INDIA

Hark the tramp of marching numbers,
India, waking from her slumbers,
    Calls us to the fray.

Not with weapons slaughter dealing,
Not with blood her triumph sealing,
But with peace-bells loudly pealing,
  Dawns her Freedom's Day.

Justice is her buckler stainless,
Argument her rapier painless,
  Truth her pointed lance.
Hark! her song to Heaven ringing,
Hatreds all behind her flinging,
Peace and joy to all she's bringing,
  Love her shining glance.

Mother, Devī! all-victorious,
Thou hast seen a vision glorious,
  Dreamt of Liberty.
Now the vision has its ending
In the truth, all dreams transcending,
Hope and fact together blending,
  Free! from sea to sea.

By thy plains and snow-clad mountains,
By thy streams and rushing fountains,
  By Himālayan heights,
By the past of splendid story,
By the hopes of future glory,
By the strength of wisdom hoary,
  Claim thy sacred Rights.

And she claimed them.

CHAPTER IV

THE GREAT AGITATION *(Continued)*

BOMBAY, LUCKNOW, AND THE HOME RULE LEAGUES

WHEN the Congress met at Bombay, 1915, Sir Saṭyenḍra Sinha in the chair, it was, so far as the bulk of the delegates were concerned a Home Rule Congress, throbbing with life and new energy. But the older men, the leaders, as said above, did not wish that a separate organisation should be formed, as they thought it would weaken the Congress. We had a meeting of leading adherents of the two parties, and agreed that if the Congress had not started an educative propaganda by August 31st, 1916, a Home Rule League might be started. Many of those who followed my programme were angry with me for yielding so far to the wishes of the older men, especially as Mr. Ḍadabhai Naoroji had approved the idea. I felt, however, that we could afford to wait eight months for the sake of union, and that it was not for me, a new-comer into the Congress—having attended it for the first time in 1914—to go against the older men, who had borne the burden and heat of the day. I managed therefore to restrain my more enthusiastic followers, with the result that all agreed to the resolution to form a definite scheme, as suggested the year before.

Resolution XIX, on Self-Government, was introduced, says the Anglo-Indian *Madras Mail*, "amidst scenes of great enthusiasm, the speakers being repeatedly cheered, notably the Hon. Mr. Surendranath Bannerji, Mrs. Besant, and the Hon Paṇdiṭ Madan Mohan Malaviya". The Resolution was as follows:

"That this Congress is of opinion that the time has arrived to introduce further and substantial measures of reform towards the attainment of Self-Government as defined in Article I of the Constitution, namely reforming and liberalising the system of Government in this country so as to secure to the people an effective control over it by amongst others:

(*a*) the introduction of Provincial Autonomy including financial independence;

(*b*) expansion and reform of the Legislative Councils so as to make them truly and adequately representative of all sections of the people and to give them effective control over the acts of the Executive Government;

(*c*) the reconstruction of the various Executive Councils and the establishment of similar Executive Councils in Provinces where they do not exist;

(*d*) the reform or the abolition of the Council of the Secretary of State for India;

(*e*) establishment of Legislative Councils in Provinces where they do not now exist;

(*f*) the readjustment of the relations between the Secretary of State for India and the Government of India; and;

(*g*) a liberal measure of Local Self-Government.

That this Congress authorises the All-India Congress Committee to frame a scheme of reform and a programme of continuous work, educative and propagandist, having regard to the principles embodied in this Resolution, and further authorises the said Committee to confer with the Committee that may be appointed by the All-India Muslim League for the same purpose, and to take such further measures as may be necessary; the said Committee to submit its report on or before the 1st September, 1916, to the General Secretaries, who shall circulate it to the different Provincial Congress Committees as early as possible."

This Resolution bore its fruit in "the Congress-League Scheme," carried in the Lucknow Congress of 1916 by the united parties in the Congress and by the All-India Muslim League. It gave a good programme for the work of 1916, in addition to the before-named propaganda. The Provincial Congress Committees worked separately, and their work was submitted to the All-India Congress Committee, and was thus thoroughly discussed before the latter met the Council of the Muslim League, and came to an agreement with it on all points, including the burning question of Muslim representation. The decision on this was accepted later by the British Government, and was incorporated in the Reform Act.

I wrote from Bombay on December 29, 1915, to *New India*, a letter in which the following occurred:

> I expect as this resolution has been carried, the Home Rule League will not be sanctioned this evening. The opportunity of joint action on a common platform between Hindūs and Muslims will thus be destroyed. I am, of course, bound by my promise not to start the organisation if the Indian leaders disapprove it, deep as will be the disappointment felt all over the country by the rank and file, who have come to the Congress with the object of joining it. They must console themselves with the fact that the strength of the delegates in favour of a constitutional agitation to be begun at once, and carried on through the year, has forced even the timid to agree to a resolution ordering the All-India Congress Committee to form a programme for such educative work. I hope we shall hear no more about "embarrassing the Government," now that the Congress, under the cautious Presidentship of Sir Saṭyendra P. Sinha, has ordered this propaganda to be carried on. (*New India*, December 31, 1915, p. 11.)

And again in *New India* of January 6, 1916 (p. 10):

As regards the suspension of the formation of the H. R. L., the position is really quite clear. I had said from the beginning that it was intended to strengthen, not to weaken, the Congress. I had further said, in a note *addressed to every signatory*, that I would not organise the League if the Indian leaders were against it. The enthusiasm raised by the brief three months' work brought a huge number of delegates to the Congress; the resolution which was carried took up the proposed work of the H. R. L.—my resolution on the 27th December was: "To establish a Home Rule League to carry on an educative propaganda throughout the country"—and adopted, after that meeting, the mandate to the All-India Congress Committee to frame a programme for continuous educational propaganda. I had to choose, on the 29th, between obeying this mandate as a member of the All-India Congress Committee, or starting a new organisation to do exactly the same thing, creating a split for the mere sake of leading a new body when the old one had taken up the work. All the well-known Congress leaders were against the formation of a new body under the changed conditions, and my own judgment agreed with theirs. For I should have had to lead the young men into a propaganda without the protection of the elders which I had sought to gain for them, and I, alone, should have been unable to protect them. It would have been madness to do this, when they could do exactly the same work under the ægis of the Congress. The formation was therefore adjourned. If the All-India Congress Committee does not carry out the mandate of the Congress, and if the Congress organisation goes to sleep, then we can go on with our adjourned meeting. But we have no right to insult the trusted men elected by the Congress Circles by assuming that they will disobey the Congress. In Madras, we are already beginning, within one week of our return, and I have no doubt that other Circles will do the same.

If we are to win Home Rule, union is absolutely necessary: the Right and Left Wings of the National Party are united by the Congress; the Congress and the Muslim League have appointed Committees to confer with each other on a scheme of reform, and it rests with us to make Reform and Home Rule identical. Would it have been right, at this critical moment, to play into the hands of the strong party opposed to Indian Self-Government by insisting on a separate movement, a separate label for identical work, yielding to the fissiparous tendency which is the curse of India? Is it not better for us all to sacrifice personalities to principles, names to facts, and, rejoicing that the National Congress has taken the work we proposed to do as an auxiliary, into its own hand, joyfully and loyally to labour to make its work a success, as it will be if we throw all our enthusiasm and energy into the propaganda it has ordered.

The Resolution, with a summary of the most important speeches, was published as "Home Rule Series, No 1"; "Published for the Editorial Board of the All-India Self-Government Propaganda Fund, by Annie Besant" was the legend on its title-page. It was the first of 31 tracts, of which the first 16 were published by the Board. The names of the Editorial Board may be put on record: they were:

BENGAL: Hirendranāṭh Ḍaṭṭa. A. Rasul. J. Chouḍhuri. BOMBAY: Jamnaḍās Ḍwarkāḍās. Raṭansi Morarji. Umar Sobani. MADRAS: Annie Besant. C. P. Rāmaswāmi Aiyar. B. P. Wadia. UNITED PROVINCES: Tej Bahāḍūr Sapru. C. Y. Chinṭāmani. Wazir Hasan. BIHAR: Mazar-ul-Haque. Parmeshwar Lāll. Moozam Ali Khan.

Members of the Board do not necessarily agree with every page in a pamphlet, but think it, as a whole, useful and worthy of publication.

They were the younger leaders of the then National Party, energetic and determined to work. This was the least aggressive way in which the propaganda for Home Rule could be carried on, while arousing and educating the country, and was added to the work begun in 1915 and continued through 1916 and 1917, so that the volume of propaganda literature grew ever greater during these years.

The year 1916 opened under good auspices. I wrote in *The Commonweal* of January 7, 1916 (p. 2):

> The time for piecemeal reforms is over, and the Congress marches steadily forward under the banner of Self-Government. It is absolutely essential that the propaganda proposed for the Home Rule League and adopted by the Congress, shall go forward actively. Mr. C. Y. Chinṭāmani began it nobly with his brilliant lecture on Self-Government in Poona, with Mr. Bāl Gaṅgāḍhār Ṭilak in the chair—the combination proclaiming the reunion of the Right and Left Wings of the National party—a necessary preliminary to successful action. Mr. Chinṭāmani, we are sure, will do his part in the U. P. We in Madras are planning our campaign, and we should soon hear from Bihar and from Lucknow. Sindh, we know, is eager for work. The popular propaganda can be carried on upon the broad lines we are already agreed upon, while we prepare the more detailed plan for Easter.

The reunion spoken of was brought about as related in a letter to *New India*, which appeared on December 31, 1915, p. 11:

A matter of great rejoicing is the closing of the breach between the two wings of the National Party, and the declaration that it is not necessary that a delegate should be a member of a Congress Committee in order that he should be elected—thus forbidding any unfair order such as the one by the Bombay Provincial Congress in order to shut out people they disliked. We shall have a United Congress at Lucknow, the first since the Surat split; the wound has been healed, and what Madras began, Bombay has completed. Let us now all work together for the common Motherland, and be rivals only in devotion to her.

In that same number, in "India and Great Britain," I wrote (p. 3):

Great and epoch-making is the point in the joint history at which India and England have now arrived, and on their attitude to each other and on the decisions that will be come to at the end of the War, hang mighty issues, affecting the welfare and happiness of yet unborn generations in both lands. We may well spend the months which lie before us, ere the War can end, and the terms of peace can be so settled between the belligerents that there is breathing-time for other problems to be handled, in considering carefully and deeply the many-sided questions which must arise over the re-settlement of the relation of India to Great Britain.

The question of Home Rule for India has now been brought within the sphere of "practical politics"; the great demonstration by the Congress, and the plain-spoken declarations of the President of the Muslim League meeting, have brought it to the front; from all parts of India delegates flocked to acclaim it, and the Congress has been revitalised and placed in the van of the Nation by the enthusiasm aroused by the cry of Home Rule. Never again will it be possible for anyone to declare on the Congress platform that Indian Self-Government is a far-off vision, for it has descended from the world of ideals into the world of acts.

After pointing out that the preparation of the Congress Scheme must be accompanied by "a programme for educational propaganda during the year," so that the people might be competent to discuss the details put before them in the Scheme, I urged that each Congress Circle should prepare leaflets and pamphlets to aid this propaganda. Further, I pleaded that Home Rule would remove the *causes* of

India's poverty by "altering the system which breeds the poverty" (p. 3):

> If India is, as is so often pointed out, the most poverty-stricken country in the world, there must be a cause for this. If the most poverty-stricken country in the world is also the most costly Government in the world, there is obviously a need for retrenchment. If Indian interests are subordinated to the interests not only of Lancashire, but until lately of Germany, and now of Japan, it is clear that we need a system of administration which will put India's interests first. Hence, if India is to live, her own children must take up the duties of Government, and administer their own affairs. The time has come of which Macaulay prophesied, when India shall be Free and Self-Governing.

Returning to the same subject the following week I showed why "For Great Britain's sake India should have Home Rule." (*Ibid.*, January 14, p. 23.) How much stronger would England have been, had she taken the advice of the country given thirty years before by introducing a system of Indian volunteers. If she had had Home Rule, then

> when the war broke out, India would have ready, and would have sprung to arms, with all the pride

of a race conscious of its freedom, to defend the Empire in which she was a partner, to make Egypt and the Suez Canal as safe as the centre of England. The War would have been over in a few weeks, if indeed it had ever begun, with the millions of a free and armed India standing forward to protect the Empire.

For when Home Rule has obliterated the sad memories of the past, and when Indians in England and Englishmen in India meet as equals, as citizens, as welcome residents in each other's countries, in the mutual respect and trust that can only grow out of equal freedom, then indeed shall they be sharers in an Empire, peaceful, free, and prosperous. Then shall they be knit together by ties of love that nothing can rend asunder. Then shall East and West understand each other, hand clasped in hand, clear eyes shining on each other in mutual friendship, mutual helpfulness. Then shall the designs of Providence in bringing them together be no longer inscrutable, for they shall form an Empire that none shall dare to threaten, an Empire that shall be the home of Liberty, the Guardian of weak Nations, the terror of the would-be oppressor, the glorious home of Science, of Literature, of Art, an Empire which shall unite East and West, in which, "Righteousness and Peace shall have kissed each other". (*Ibid.*, January 14, p. 23.)

If the year 1916 marked the beginning of a new phase in the struggle for Liberty, it also saw the beginning of a new form of resistance to it. The growing strength of the Home Rule movement during the autumn of 1915 alarmed the Government of Madras, which possessed, perhaps, the most reactionary of the Civilian class in its Executive Council and bureaucratic Government, and Lord Pentland, the then Governor, was pliant in their hands—a well-meaning but weak man.

They determined on repression, and the Press Act, the Act which placed every newspaper at the mercy of the Local Government was invoked. On May 26, 1916, notice was served on *New India*, and a security levied of Rs. 2,000, paid on June 5. It was the first step of the Pentland Government on the path that led quickly to the Reform Act of 1919. Incidentally, the first Court of the Hindū University, of which I was a member, took place on August 12 of the same year. Naturally, the levy of security could make no difference in the well-considered policy of *New India*, and the security was forfeited on August 28, and a new security of Rs. 10,000 levied. The Act stated that the security might be given in Government Promissory Notes, or in cash; the Government refused the Notes and insisted on the cash. When the Press Bill was before the Council, the Law Officer, Mr. Sinha, had promised that interest should always be paid on the money taken as security, saying that it was always invested, and therefore interest accrued. The Madras Government, however, did not feel itself bound by the pledge of the Government of India; it refused the Government paper, insisted on cash, and some of its agents put the interest into the Government treasury, thus levying on *New India* a continuing fine of Rs. 350 a year, reckoning interest at the low figure of 3½ per cent. Such were the pleasant little ways of the Madras Government at that time.

Being a fighter against oppression, I continued to edit *New India* on the same lines, and began an action against the Government for the recovery of the forfeited security.

I knew it was a hopeless task from the beginning, as the Press Act was so worded that no one penalised by the Executive under it could possibly escape, as had been pointed out by Sir Lawrence Jenkins, the Chief Justice of the Calcutta High Court. But in fighting bad law, every opportunity must be seized, so beginning with a Special Bench in the Madras Court (September 27, 1916) I fought on to the Privy Council. Mr. C. P. Rāmaswāmi Aiyar made a fine effort on a technical legal point, but could not carry it. The Acting Chief Justice acquitted me of all sedition and admitted my perfect loyalty to the Crown, but, like his peer in the Calcutta Court, he thought some of the articles came within the Act.

This all made good propaganda, and educated the people to understand the benefits of bureaucratic rule. The advantage of going on to the Privy Council was that it tied up the bureaucratic hands, while *New India* though under heavy security and liable to have the press forfeited after a second forfeiture of the security, could go on upon its unrepentant way until the first security case was finally decided.

Two Home Rule Leagues were formed during the year 1916. Mr. Tilak formed one and I the other, on the ground that some people loved him and hated me, and others hated him and loved me; hence working-together-separately was the best policy. We of the Congress of 1915 formed our All-India Home Rule League in September 1, 1916, according to the agreement reached in Bombay at Christmas, 1915. It worked splendidly and successfully through the remaining months of 1916, through 1917 and 1918.

A "Home Rule (English Auxiliary) League" was formed in England during 1916, and in fact, it preceded ours. It worked most actively in Britain, representing the wish of India for Freedom within the Empire, printed and circulated large numbers of pamphlets, and created in England so lively an interest in India that the Government there looked on it suspiciously, without the smallest reason, unless it were that after the Government had persuaded the publishers in England of a little sixpenny book of mine, called *India—A Nation*, to withdraw it from circulation, the English Auxiliary printed a pretty half-crown edition of it, and sent it to every member of Parliament. Muriel, Countess De La Warr, Miss Barbara Villiers, Mr. George Lansbury—before the days of "direct action"—and Mr. John Scurr, were the most prominent members of it.

At the Congress of 1916, at Lucknow, we had a splendid gathering. At many meetings through the year we had hammered out our Scheme, as said above, and it was passed both by the Congress and the Muslim League.

Misfortunes make strange bed-fellows, and the Madras Government, casting about for a new weapon against the irrepressible Home Rulers—who continued their constitutional struggle for Reforms and had now a Congress-League Scheme which they were bent on popularising—formed by some of its members an alliance with Dr. Nair, a powerful writer with a savage pen, and, regarding the Home Rule movement as chiefly among Brāhmaṇas, pre-eminently the intelligentsia of the country and predominant among Congress leaders, it was resolved to stir up the Non-Brāhmaṇas—who included most of the great landlords and the wealthy merchant class, as well as a majority of the industrial workers—against the Brāhmaṇas. The landlords and rich merchants were even more rigid—being more rarely English-educated—in their exclusion of lower caste Hindūs and outcastes than the Brāhmaṇas. In fact, the leaders in the uplift of the submerged classes were mostly Brāhmaṇas, and especially on the West Coast, where outcastes were treated worse than elsewhere, the Brāhmaṇas led the crusade in which—touched by the spirit of Liberty—the outcastes began to establish their right to use all public roads like other citizens; in fact a great memorial against such use was sent up by "high-class non-Brāhmaṇas" to Lord Pentland, when the outcastes, led by a Brāhmaṇa, walked in procession through a road which the petitioners tried to keep shut against them. When we returned from the Lucknow Congress of 1916, we found the results of the non-Brāhmaṇa movement already marked. It had declared itself against Home Rule, supported the British autocracy, and began a furious attack on all who desired to win political freedom within the British Empire.

In *New India*, January 22, 1917, p. 5, a report is given of a meeting of the newly formed South Indian People's Association. The movement was then, said Rao Bahāḍūr P. Theagaraya Chetty, only a month old, but they had already Rs. 36,000, and were sure of getting the lakh they wanted to start a paper in a short time. It was a wealthy party. Mr. Kaṇḍasāwmi Cheṭṭy said:

> Government by the people meant that they should have a body of intelligent people. Were they in a position to have Government by the people? Would they prefer to be governed by a typical Englishman, or a typical Brāhmaṇa? The Englishman was a selfish creature. He was a mercantile being, but he had also ideals of freedom, justice and fairplay. So he would rather throw himself on the mercy of the liberty-loving Englishman, than of an oligarchy which played upon the people and their weakness. Their Home Rule meant Anti-Foreign Rule. He could not bring himself to think that an Englishman was a common enemy. He might be an enemy of the Brāhmaṇas,

but certainly he was not an enemy of the Non-Brāhmaṇas. Non-Brāhmaṇas did not look upon the Government or Englishmen as enemies.

Thus began the Hymn of Hate against a small but brilliantly intellectual and cultured class; it became a vendetta, a crusade by rank, wealth, and numbers against a class for the most part poor, but highly educated; for the Brāhmaṇas, traditionally learned, had grasped at English education, and had thereby risen to posts in which high intellectual ability and knowledge of English were required, while the bulk of the poor of that caste crowded the Government subordinate offices, on miserable salaries as clerks, translators, etc.

The speech was typical not only in its hate but in its misrepresentation. It will be seen from the preceding extracts that the Reformers did not hate the English, though they fought the Bureaucracy that denied liberty to the Nation. Constantly they put forward the

English ideals of Liberty, and urged a reform of the system of Government for England's sake as well as for India's. The whole Home Rule movement was designed to benefit both countries, and one of the objects of the All-India Home Rule League was to strengthen the British connection and to win the status of a Free Nation as part of a Commonwealth of Free Nations under the British Crown. Home Rulers recognised that Home Rule was a condition of preserving the British connection.

The alliance between members of the Madras Government and the non-Brāhmaṇa, or rather anti-Brāhmaṇa, crusade was shown by the presence of Sir Alexander Cardew at a meeting held in Madras on November 24, 1917, when Dr. Nair, Rao Bahāḍūr P. Ṭheagaraya Cheṭṭy, K. Venkaṭa Reḍḍi Naiḍu and R. Venkaṭaraṭnam Naiḍu, with the Director of Public Instruction were present, to welcome the non-Brāhmaṇa graduates of the year, and Dr. Nair emphasised the interest taken by Sir Alexander in Dravidian graduates. Sir Alexander expressed the hope that there would be many, more, and *New India* wrote:

> The presence of Sir Alexander Cardew at the above gathering requires notice. He must have known that the Association which he patronised was a separatist one; it is in fact the parent of the body now working mischief as the Liberal Federation. That Sir Alexander Cardew should have so prominently associated himself with that body, and that too in a distinctly sectarian function, is a matter to be considered by the general public. Supporters are being canvassed for such new movements on the plea that its members can expect at any time to bask in official sunshine; and the task of such canvassers is very considerably facilitated by the open way in which high officials of the Government associate with them. The next step will probably be a public appeal by similarly placed gentlemen to join the new movement, or to supply funds to it. Incidents of this type indicate to what undignified lengths persons are now prepared to go in thwarting our National aspirations. (*Loc. cit.*, November 26, 1917.

Thus fostered, the movement spread rapidly, and proved to be a veritable sower of the dragon-seeds of hatred against the small class of Brāhmaṇas among the people of the Presidency; later, it was naturally followed by bitter attacks from the outcastes against all who were caste-men.

The early months of 1917—so far as we were concerned—were passed in active propaganda, popularising the Congress-League Scheme. On the other hand, Lord Pentland took occasion to say that in the Legislative Council:

> All thoughts of the early grant of Responsible Self-Government should be put entirely out of mind. (*New India*, May 25, 1917, p. 4).

That was impossible, and we went on with our work. Then came a blow which was intended to put a sudden end to the work of the paper, then regarded as the chief advocate of Home Rule; *New India*—as it would not stop for securities—should be stopped by the internment of its Editor, its Assistant Editor, and its liveliest and most pungent contributor—Annie Besant, B. P. Wadia and G. S. Arundale. An order of internment was issued with a few days grace; that executed, the press could be sequestered and all would be well. It was served on June 16, the day after the anniversary of the signing of Magna Carta in 1215. No reason was assigned, and we never learnt what was our exact offence. Lord Pentland called me to see him, but refused any information. I suspended *New India* on June 18th, in order to save the security and the press, sold the Vasanṭā Press to Rai Sāhab G. Soobbiah Cheṭṭy, and recovered its Rs. 5,000 security on June 19; on June 20, I sold *The Commonweal* Press to Mr. Raṅga Reḍḍi, and the *New India* Press to Mr. P. K. Telang, recovering Rs. 2,000 and Rs. 10,000, and issued a notice to *New India* subscribers; the paper appeared again on the 21st; it was quick work, but the time was short, and I had to "hustle". So we had three bran new press-owners, under securities of only Rs. 2,000 each, instead of Rs. 17,000. I do not think that the Press Act was intended to have a motor-car, driven by a lady of nearly seventy, rushed through it in this way, like the proverbial "coach and horses". But then it was drawn up by bureaucrats who had had no experience of Home Rulers; they were accustomed to revolutionaries and even passive resisters, but had never met with constitutional fighters for Liberty, who regarded them with amused unconcern, and perfect good temper. Before we left, Mr. Horniman and Mr. Kelkar kindly came over from Bombay and Poona to offer help, and each wrote an article for *New India* of the 21st; as they were already editors, we thought it was better that Mr. P. K. Telang should assume charge of *New India*, and he promptly filled the gap. He forfeited the security in due course, and another Rs. 10,000 was levied. When I resumed the editorship, Mr. Telang presented the press to Mr. Raṅga Reḍḍi, who started again with another Rs. 2,000. The magistrate however most improperly kept the Rs. 10,000 on various excuses for over a year, but when another magistrate took his place, the money was at once refunded. The long fight made good propaganda, and helped Home Rule immensely.

For when we, the interned, foregathered at Ootacamund, a whirlwind broke out, raged up and down the country, stormed over to Britain, Russia, France, America, at several hundred miles an hour. Questions were asked in the House of Commons and in the Viceroy's Legislative Council. Members of Parliament, like the babes in the wood, were snowed over with leaves—of paper. "Who would have thought," said a very high official pensively, "that there would have been such a fuss about one old woman?" Crowds of people and many popular leaders joined the Home Rule League. Meetings were held, resolutions flew about; C. P. Rāmaswāmi Aiyar, Jamnaḍās Ḍwārkaḍās, Congressmen everywhere, fanned the storm and rode it. They preserved perfect order; never a window was broken; never a riot occurred; never a policeman was assaulted; never man, woman or child went to gaol. For three months the vehement agitation continued unbrokenly, without ever breaking a law, and the students who wanted to strike were kept in their schools and colleges, and then—came the declaration of August 20, 1917, that the goal of Great Britain in India was Responsible Government, and an announcement that the Secretary of State for India was coming thither, to learn the wishes of the people. To "obtain a calm atmosphere" the three internees were to be liberated.

It was a truly constitutional triumph, won by a United India, and was crowned by the election of the Home Rule President as President of the National Congress of 1917.

Mr. Montagu, the Secretary of State, came to India, and travelled with the Viceroy, Lord Chelmsford, all over India, meeting Deputations representing every type of political opinion. The National Congress and the Muslim League, and the two Home Rule Leagues presented at Delhi on November 26, 1917, memorials asking for Home Rule. The National Congress and the League were represented by a Joint Deputation from their respective Executives, and the memorial was read by Mr. Surenḍranāth Bannerji. After a careful and argumentative presentation of the Indian case, it wound up:

> We submit that the reforms for which the National Congress and the Muslim League plead, are needed as much in the interests of the good government of the country and the happiness and

prosperity of the people as for the legitimate satisfaction of our National self-respect and for a due recognition of India's place among the free and civilised Nations of the Empire and the outside world. Nor are they less necessary to strengthen and solidify the British connection with this ancient land. India has given freely of her love and service to England, and she aspires to attain to her proper place of equality and honour in the Commonwealth of Nations, which are proud to own fidelity to his Imperial Majesty the King-Emperor. If, as has been said, the British Empire is the greatest secular power on earth making for the good of mankind, India is hopeful and confident that she will not be denied what is in every way due to her, especially after this great War of Liberty, in which it has been authoritatively recognised that she has played a distinguished and honourable part.

The two Home Rule Leagues were represented by Mr. Tilak and myself respectively and we also read our memorials. At Madras, the All-India Home Rule League presented Mr. Montagu with a million verified signatures, gathered in the Presidency, and conveyed to him in three or four carts.

It was the end of a strenuous struggle of three crowded years ; to me the end of another stage in twenty-four years of steady labour ; to the Congress the end of one stage in its thirty-three years of political efforts for liberty.

Thenceforth Liberty's battle entered on another phase.

CHAPTER V

THE NEW SPIRIT IN INDIA

WRITING at the end of 1917, I sketched out what seemed to me to be the Causes of what I called "the New Spirit in India". It was part of my speech as President of the National Congress, the post which, since 1885, had been regarded as the highest place within the Nation's gift, the proof of her fullest confidence and love. Reading that sketch to-day, in 1922, I do not feel that I can better it, so I use it here, and it has the advantage of marking the place held at the end of 1917 by the National Movement in India, as seen by one who was among the leaders in that struggle which had ended in triumph. [*Here begins the reprint*].

Apart from the natural exchange of thought between East and West, the influence of English education, literature and ideals, the effect of travel in Europe, Japan and the United States of America, and other recognised causes for the changed outlook in India, there have been special forces at work during the last few years to arouse a New Spirit in India, and to alter her attitude of mind. These may be summed up as:

(*a*) The Awakening of Asia.

(*b*) Discussions abroad on Alien Rule and Imperial Reconstruction.

(*c*) Loss of Belief in the Superiority of the White Races.

(*d*) The Awakening of the Merchants.

(*e*) The Awakening of the Women to claim their Ancient Position.

(*f*) The Awakening of the Masses.

Each of these causes has had its share in the splendid change of attitude in the Indian

Nation, in the uprising of a spirit of pride of country, of independence, of self-reliance, of dignity, of self-respect. The War has quickened the rate of evolution of the world, and no country has experienced the quickening more than our Motherland.

(a) *The Awakening of Asia*

In a conversation I had with Lord Minto, soon after his arrival as Viceroy, he discussed the so-called "unrest in India," and recognised it as the inevitable result of English Education, of English Ideals of Democracy, of the Japanese victory over Russia, and of the changing conditions in the outer world. I was therefore not surprised to read his remark that he recognised, "frankly and publicly, that new aspirations were stirring in the hearts of the people, that they were part of a larger movement common to the whole East, and that it was necessary to satisfy them to a reasonable extent by giving them a larger share in the administration".

But the present movement in India will be very poorly understood, if it be regarded only in connection with the movement in the East. The awakening of Asia is part of a world-movement, which has been quickened into marvellous rapidity by the World War. The world-movement is towards Democracy, and for the West dates from the breaking away of the American Colonies from Great Britain, consummated in 1776, and its sequel in the French Revolution of 1789. Needless to say that its root was in the growth of modern science undermining the fabric of intellectual servitude, in the work of the Encyclopædists, and in that of Jean-Jacques Rousseau and of Thomas Paine. In the East, the swift changes in Japan, the success of the Japanese Empire against Russia, the downfall of the Manchu dynasty in China and the establishment of a

Chinese Republic, the efforts at improvement in Persia, hindered by the interference of Russia and Great Britain with her growing ambition, and the creation of British and Russian "spheres of influence," depriving her of her just liberty, and now the Russian Revolution and the probable rise of a Russian Republic in Europe and Asia, have all entirely changed the conditions before existing in India. Across Asia, beyond the Himālayas, stretch free and self-ruling Nations. India no longer sees as her Asian neighbours the huge domains of a Tsar and a Chinese despot, and compares her condition under British rule with those of their subject populations. British rule profited by the comparison, at least until 1905, when the great period of repression set in. But in future, unless India wins Self-Government, she will look enviously at her Self-Governing neighbours, and the contrast will intensify her unrest.

But even if she gains Home Rule, as I believe she will, her position in the Empire will imperatively demand that she shall be strong as well as free. She becomes not only a vulnerable point in the Empire, as the Asian Nations evolve their own ambitions and rivalries, but also a possession to be battled for. Mr. Laing once said: "India is the milch-cow of England," a Kāmaḍhenu, in fact, a "cow of plenty"; and if that view should arise in Asia, the ownership of the milch-cow would become a matter of dispute, as of old between Vashishtha and Vishvāmiṭra. Hence India must be capable of self-defence both by land and sea. There may be a struggle for the primacy of Asia, for supremacy in the Pacific, for the mastery of Australasia, to say nothing of the inevitable trade-struggles, in which Japan is already endangering Indian industry and Indian trade, while India is unable to protect herself.

In order to face these larger issues with equanimity, the Empire requires a contented, strong, self-dependent and armed India, able to hold her own and to aid the Dominions, especially Australia, with her small population and immense unoccupied and undefended area. India alone has the man-power which can effectively maintain the Empire in Asia, and it is a short-sighted, a criminally short-sighted, policy not to build up her strength as a Self-Governing State within the Commonwealth of Free Nations under the British Crown. The Englishmen in India talk loudly of their interests; what can this mere handful do to protect their interests against attack in the coming years? Only in a free and powerful India will they be safe. Those who read Japanese papers know how strongly, even during the War, they parade unchecked their pro-German sympathies, and how likely after the War is an alliance between these two ambitious and warlike Nations. Japan will come out of the War with her army and navy unweakened, and her trade immensely strengthened. Every consideration of sane statesmanship should lead Great Britain to trust India more than Japan, so that the British Empire in Asia may rest on the sure foundation of Indian loyalty, the loyalty of a free and contented people, rather than be dependent on the continued friendship of a possible future rival. For international friendships are governed by National interests, and are built on quicksands, not on rock.

Englishmen in India must give up the idea that English dominance is necessary for the protection of their interests, amounting, in 1915, to £365,399,000 sterling. They do not claim to dominate the United States of America, because they have invested there £688,078,000. They do not claim to dominate the Argentine Republic, because they have invested there £269,808,000. Why then should they claim to dominate India on the ground of their investments? Britons must give up the idea that India is a possession to be exploited for their own benefit, and must see her as a friend, an equal, a Self-Governing Dominion within the Empire, a Nation like themselves, a willing partner in the Empire, but not a dependent. The democratic movement in Japan, China and Russia in Asia has sympathetically affected India, and it is idle to pretend that it will cease to affect her.

(b) *Discussions Abroad on Alien Rule and Reconstruction*

But there are other causes which have been working in India, consequent on the British attitude against autocracy and in defence of freedom in Europe, while her attitude to India has, until lately, been left in doubt. Therefore

I spoke of a splendid opportunity lost. India at first believed whole-heartedly that Great Britain was fighting for the freedom of all Nationalities. Even now, Mr. Asquith declared —in his speech in the House of Commons reported here last October, on the peace resolution of Mr. Ramsay Macdonald—that "the Allies are fighting for nothing but freedom," and, an important addition—"for nothing short of freedom". In his speech declaring that Britain would stand by France in her claim for the restoration of Alsace-Lorraine, he spoke of "the intolerable degradation of a foreign yoke". Is such a yoke less intolerable, less wounding to self-respect, here than in Alsace-Lorraine, where the rulers and the ruled are both of European blood, similar in religion and habits? As the War went on, India slowly and unwillingly came to realise that the hatred of autocracy was confined to autocracy in the West, and that the degradation was only regarded as intolerable for men of white races; that freedom was lavishly promised to all except to India; that new powers were to be given to the Dominions, but not to India. India was markedly left out of the speeches of statesmen dealing with the future of the Empire, and at last there was plain talk of the White Empire, the Empire of the Five Nations, and the "coloured races" were lumped together as the wards of the White Empire, doomed to an indefinite minority.

The peril was pressing; the menace unmistakable. The Reconstruction of the Empire was on the anvil; what was to be India's place therein? The Dominions were proclaimed as partners; was India to remain a Dependency? Mr. Bonar Law bade the Dominions strike while the iron was hot; was India to wait till it was cold? India saw her soldiers fighting for freedom in Flanders, in France, in Gallipoli, in Asia Minor, in China, in Africa; was she to have no share of the freedom for which she fought? At last she sprang to her feet and cried, in the words of one of her noblest sons: "Freedom is my birthright; and I want it." The words "Home Rule" became her Manṭram. She claimed her place in the Empire.

Thus, while she continued to support, and even to increase, her army abroad, fighting for the Empire, and poured out her treasures as water for Hospital Ships, War Funds, Red Cross Organisations, and the gigantic War Loan, a dawning fear oppressed her, lest, if she did not take order with her own household, success in the War for the Empire might mean decreased liberty for herself.

The recognition of the right of the Indian Government to make its voice heard in Imperial matters, when they were under discussion in an Imperial Conference, was a step in the right direction. But disappointment was felt that while other countries were represented by responsible Ministers, the representation in India's case was of the Government, of a Government irresponsible to her, and not the representative of herself. No fault was found with the choice itself, but only with the non-representative character of the chosen, for they were selected by the Government, and not by the elected members of the Supreme Council. This defect in the resolution moved by the Hon. Khān Bahāḍūr M. M. Shāfi on October 2, 1915, was pointed out by the Hon. Mr. Surenḍranāṭh Bannerji. He said:

> My Lord, in view of a situation so full of hope and promise, it seems to me that my friend's Resolution does not go far enough. He pleads for *official* representation at the Imperial Conterence: he does not plead for *popular* representation. He urges that an address be presented to His Majesty's Government, through the Secretary of State for India, for official representation at the Imperial Council. My Lord, official representation may mean little or nothing. It may indeed be attended with

some risk; for I am sorry to have to say—but say it I must—that our officials do not always see eye to eye with us as regards many great public questions which affect this country; and indeed their views, judged from our standpoint, may sometimes seem adverse to our interests. At the same time, my Lord, I recognise the fact that the Imperial Conference is an assemblage of officials pure and simple, consisting of Ministers of the United Kingdom and of the Self-Governing Colonies. But, my Lord, there is an essential difference between them and ourselves. In their case, the Ministers are the elect of the people, their organ and their voice, answerable to them for their conduct and their proceedings. In our case, our officials are public servants in name, but in reality they are the masters of the public. The situation may improve, and I trust it will, under the liberalising influence of your Excellency's beneficent administration; but we must take things as they are, and not indulge in building castles in the air which may vanish "like the baseless fabric of a vision".

It was said to be an epoch-making event that "Indian Representatives" took part in the Conference. Representatives they were, but, as said, of the British Government in India, not of India, whereas their colleagues represented their Nations. They did good work, none the less, for they were able and experienced men, though they failed us in the Imperial Preference Conference, and, partially, on the Indentured Labour question. Yet we hope that the presence in the Conference of men of Indian birth may prove to be the proverbial "thin end of the wedge," and may have convinced their colleagues that, while India was still a Dependency, India's sons were fully their equals.

The Report of the Public Services Commission, though now too obviously obsolete to be discussed, caused both disappointment and resentment; for it showed that, in the eyes of the majority of the Commissioners, English domination in Indian administration was to be perpetual, and that 30 years hence she would only hold a pitiful 25 per cent of the higher appointments in the I.C.S. and the Police. I cannot, however, mention that Commission, even in passing, without voicing India's thanks to the Hon. Mr. Justice Rahīm, for his rare courage in writing a solitary Minute of Dissent, in which he totally rejected the Report, and laid down the right principles which should govern recruitment for the Indian Civil Services.

India had but three representatives on the Commission; G. K. Gokhale died ere it made its Report, his end quickened by his sufferings during its work, by the humiliation of the way in which his countrymen were treated. Of Mr. Abdur Rahīm I have already spoken. The Hon. Mr. M. B. Chaubâl signed the Report, but dissented from some of its most important recommendations. The whole Report was written "before the flood," and it is now merely an antiquarian curiosity.

India, for all these reasons, was forced to see before her a future of perpetual subordination:

the Briton rules in Great Britain, the Frenchman in France, the American in America, each Dominion in its own area, but the Indian was to rule nowhere; alone among the peoples of the world, he was not to feel his own country as his own. "Britain for the British" was right and natural; "India for the Indians" was wrong, even seditious. It must be "India for the Empire," or not even for the Empire, but "for the rest of the Empire," careless of herself. "British support for British Trade" was patriotic and proper in Britain. "Svaḍeshi goods for Indians" showed a petty and anti-Imperial spirit in India. The Indian was to continue to live perpetually, and even thankfully, as Gopāl Kṛṣhṇa Gokhale said he lived now, in "an atmosphere of inferiority," and to be proud to be a citizen (without rights) of the Empire, while its other component Nations were to be citizens (with rights) in their own countries first, and citizens of the Empire secondarily. Just as her trust in Great Britain was strained nearly to breaking point came the glad news of Mr. Montagu's appointment as Secretary of State for India, of the Viceroy's invitation to him, and of his coming to hear for himself what India wanted. It was a ray of sunshine breaking through the gloom, confidence in Great Britain revived, and glad preparation was made to welcome the coming of a friend.

The attitude of India has changed to meet the changed attitude of the Governments of India and Great Britain. But let none imagine that that consequential change of attitude connotes any change in her determination to win Home Rule. She is ready to consider terms of peace, but it must be "peace with honour," and honour in this connection means Freedom. If this be not granted, an even more vigorous agitation will begin.

(c) *Loss of Belief in the Superiority of the White Races*

The undermining of this belief dates from the spreading of the Ārya Samāj and the Theosophical Society. Both bodies sought to lead the Indian people to a sense of the value of their own civilisation, to pride in their past, creating self-respect in the present, and self-confidence in the future. They destroyed the unhealthy inclination to imitate the West in all things, and taught discrimination, the using only of what was valuable in western thought and culture, instead of a mere slavish copying of everything. Another great force was that of Swāmi Vivekānanḍa, alike in his passionate love and admiration for India, and his exposure of the evils resulting from Materialism in the West. Take the following:

Children of India, I am here to speak to you to-day about some practical things, and my object in reminding you about the glories of the past is simply this. Many times have I been told that looking into the past only degenerates and leads to nothing, and that we should look to the future. That is true. But out of the past is built the future. Look back, therefore, as far as you can, drink deep of the eternal fountains that are behind, and after that, look forward, march forward, and make India brighter, greater, much higher than she ever was. Our ancestors were great. We must recall that. We must learn the elements of our being, the blood that courses in our veins; we must have faith in that blood, and what it did in the past: and out of that faith, and consciousness of past greatness, we must build an India yet greater than what she has been.

And again:

I know for certain that millions, I say deliberately, millions, in every civilised land are waiting for the message that will save them from the hideous abyss of materialism, into which modern money-worship is driving them headlong, and many of the leaders of the new Social Movements have already discovered that Veḍânṭa in its highest form can alone spiritualise their social aspirations.

The process was continued by the admiration of Saṁskṛṭ literature expressed by European scholars and philosophers. But the effect of these was confined to the few and did not reach the many. The first great shock to their belief in white superiority came from the triumph of Japan over Russia, the facing of a huge European Power by a comparatively small eastern Nation, the exposure of the weakness and rottenness of the Russian leaders, and the contrast with their hardy virile opponents, ready to sacrifice everything for their country.

The second great shock has come from the frank brutality of German theories of the State, and their practical carrying out in the treatment of conquered districts, and the laying waste of evacuated areas in retreat. The teachings of Bismarck and their practical application in France, Flanders, Belgium, Poland and Serbia have destroyed all the glamour of the superiority of Christendom over Asia. Its vaunted civilisation is seen to be but a thin veneer, and its religion a matter of form rather than of life. Gazing from afar at the ghastly heaps of the dead and the hosts of the mutilated, at science turned into devilry, and ever inventing new tortures for rending and slaying, Asia may be forgiven for thinking that, on the whole, she prefers her own religions and her own civilisations.

But even deeper than the outer tumult of War has pierced the doubt as to the reality of the Ideals of Liberty and Nationality so loudly proclaimed by the foremost western Nations, the doubt of the honesty of their champions. Sir James Meston said truly, a short time ago, that he had never, in his long experience, known Indians in so distrustful and suspicious a mood as that which he met in them to-day. And that is so. For long years Indians have been chafing over the many breaches of promises and pledges to them that remain unredeemed. The maintenance here of a system of political repression, of coercive measures increased in number and more harshly applied since 1905, the carrying of the system to a wider extent since the War for the sanctity of treaties and for the protection of Nationalities has been going on, have deepened the mistrust. A frank and courageous statesmanship applied to the honest carrying out of large reforms too long delayed, can alone remove it. The time for political tinkering is past; the time for wise and definite changes is here.

To these deep causes must be added the comparison between the progressive policy of some of the Indian States in matters which most affect the happiness of the people, and the slow advance made under British administration. The Indian notes that this advance is made under the guidance of rulers and ministers of his own race. When he sees that the suggestions made in the People's Assembly in Mysore are fully considered and, when possible, given effect to, he realises that without the forms of power, the members exercise more real power than those in our Legislative Councils. He sees education spreading, new industries fostered, villagers encouraged to manage their own affairs and take the burden of their own responsibility, and he wonders why Indian incapacity is so much more efficient than British capacity.

Perhaps, after all, for Indians, Indian rule may be the best.

(*d*) *The Awakening of the Merchants*

Of the many forces that have created New India, the awakening of the Merchants into political life is perhaps the most potent, and the most pregnant with happy possibilities. Sir Dorab Tata, in the Industrial Conference in Bombay, 1915, advocated the yoking together of Politics and Industry. It is now coming about. Hitherto the merchants had remained immersed in their own occupations, but they were awakened by the War to the necessity of taking part in politics by finding that those very occupations were threatened with disaster by the attitude of the Government; as for instance, the refusal to lend a helping hand to industries which had been connected closely with German trade and were menaced with ruin by the War; by the refusal to aid the efforts made to replace necessaries—hitherto supplied by Germany—by the founding or financing of factories for their production at home; by the restrictions put on trade under pretext of the War, that prevented the legitimate expansion of promising branches of industry; by the absence of effort to relieve the stringency of the money market, wealthy merchants being unable to obtain cash to meet their liabilities here, because their English debtors could not transmit the money they owed; some were even obliged to sell the depreciated Government paper at heavy loss in order to maintain their credit; in other cases War Bonds were offered to them in lieu of cash for goods supplied. The details have varied in different centres, and the wealthy and independent merchants of Bombay have suffered less than the merchants of Madras, with whose difficulties I am naturally more familiar.

There, added difficulties constantly arise from the favouritism shown by the Presidency Bank to English, as compared with Indian, clients, and the absence of Indians from its Directorate, complained of for years. The anxiety felt by the merchants was largely increased by the depreciation of Government paper, and apart from the heavy losses of capital incurred when necessity forced holders to sell for cash, an uneasy feeling arose as to the stability of the Government, when its securities fell so low.

Another disturbing cause was the alienation during many years of lands and minerals to foreigners, the Government looking on with indifference.

The copra and coir industry of the West Coast had passed into German hands; struck away from them by the War, there was danger of its being absorbed by the English; happily the firm of Tata and Sons stepped in and rescued it, and it remains an Indian industry. Ten years ago, the working of the blend known as monazite, an ingredient in munitions, was absorbed by Germany. Indian mica mines became German property. Undressed hides were exported wholesale to Germany, although Mysore had shewn that they could be dressed and tanned better in Indian than in European factories, and only a little encouragement and help were needed to ensure their dressing and tanning, if not also their working, here. Instead of that, the undressed hides were bought up by Government at a price fixed by themselves, and were largely exported to be dressed, tanned and worked abroad. The Viceroy, speaking in the Supreme Council on September 5th last, stated that large orders had been given to "tanners in India," and that experimental work in tanning had yielded results which promised success on a commercial scale; he expressed the hope that, after the War, the tanning industry would undergo a great expansion for general purposes. But hide merchants are distressed by an order that hides are to be purchased at War prices, the British War Office buying them to provide with leather goods the civilian population in Britain. But what has the War Office to do with providing boots for civilians, and why should India be drained for civil as well as for military purposes? If the tanning experiments are being carried on with India's money by experts paid by India, and not by

British capitalists, then the outcome should be the property of India and enrich the people of the country, not British merchants and manufacturers settled here.

The War has turned the attention of Government to the wisdom of utilising India's immense natural resources, and the Viceroy speaks of organising these resources with "a view to making India more self-contained, and less dependent on the outer world for the supplies of manufactured goods". We heartily endorse this view. This has long been the cry from Indians, for India, with her varieties of soil and climate, can produce all the materials she needs, and with her surplus goods she can—as Phillimore said of her in the seventeenth century—"with the droppings of her soil feed distant Nations". But the East India Company first, the British Government next, and lately exploiting bodies of Imperialist Traders, have vehemently insisted that India should supply raw materials, export them for manufacture abroad, and purchase, preferably within the Empire, the goods manufactured out of them. As Macaulay pointed out, the marvellous expansion of English industry was contemporaneous with the impoverishment of India. The reversal of this policy by the present Viceroy will earn India's undying gratitude, if he fosters Indian industries and not English industries in India. A witness before the Industries Commission stated that India should raise products for use outside, that is, as the East India Company put it, become a plantation for the supply of raw materials. The Viceroy must pardon us, if previous experience has made us anxious on this point. We cannot forget that a century ago the traces of iron were found in the Central Provinces, and that nothing was done to extract the metal—England then being the world's shop for iron to her own huge profit, and not desiring a rival. It was left for Tata to seize the opportunity, and his shares of Rs. 30 are now sold at Rs. 1,180. He started a great industry, and Tata's steel is sought so largely that he cannot meet the demand. Had the iron been raised and worked here during these long years, we should not now be dependent on Britain for our machinery, the want of which cripples the efforts to found new industries and to expand old ones, in order to supply the demand caused by the necessary absorption of factories in Great Britain for War work.

The Viceroy remarks truly that previous "efforts were more sporadic than systematic," but proceeds:

> The marked success which has followed the organisation of research and demonstration work in scientific agriculture, and the assistance which has been given to the mineral industries by the Geological Survey, are striking examples that encourage a bolder policy on similar lines for the benefit of other and especially the manufacturing industries.

Here, again, we must pause to remark that some of these experiments in scientific agriculture result in efforts to meet the demands of England, rather than those of India. India works up short-stapled cotton. Especially in her hand-loom industry, short-stapled cotton suits her. Lancashire wants long-stapled, and cannot get enough from the United States and Egypt. Therefore, India should substitute long- for short-stapled cotton. We confess we do not see the *sequitur*. Nor do we find, in our study of English trade, that England, which is set up as an example to be copied, has followed self-denying ordinances, and has regulated her production so as to help foreign countries to her own detriment.

However, the War has done for India, in awakening the interest of the Government in her industries, that which the attempts of Indian patriots have failed to do. The War brought about the Industries Commission, and the need for munitions has forced industrial organisation for their production. It is for Indian merchants to see, by seizing and utilising the political weapon, that the organisation and encouragement of industries by Government—unless it be a Home Government, under their own control—does not reduce Indians to a more subordinate position than they now hold. It is this danger which is playing a great part in the fear which has caused the Awakening of the Merchants. The tea industry, for instance, is in the hands of English planters, and while incomes drawn from other agricultural profits have been taxed, incomes derived from tea—which is certainly an agricultural profit—have wholly escaped till lately. If this policy be pursued, and the fostering of industries with Indian money places the industries in foreign hands, Indians will, even more than now, be ḍubāshes, and clerks, and other employees of

English-captained firms, and will depend ever more and more on wages, driven lower and lower by increasing competition.

The industrial prospects in India are by no means discouraging, if Indians exert themselves to hold their own. Mr. Tozer, in his *British India and Its Trade*, says:

> The cotton and jute manufactures, already conducted on a large scale, offer scope for still further development. Sugar and tobacco are produced in large quantities, but both require the application of the latest scientific processes of cultivation and manufacture. Oil seeds might be crushed in India instead of being exported; while cotton seeds, as yet imperfectly utilised, can be turned to good account. Hides and skins, now largely exported raw, might be more largely tanned and dressed in India. Again, the woollen and silken fabrics manufactured in India are mostly coarse fabrics and there is scope for the production of finer goods. Although railways make their own rolling stock, they have to import wheels and axles, tyres and other iron work. At present steel is manufactured on a very small scale, and the number of iron foundries and machine shops, although increasing, is capable of greater expansion. Machinery and machine tools have for the most part to be imported. Millions of

agriculturists and artisans use rude tools which might be replaced by similar articles that are more durable and of better make. Improved oil presses and hand-looms should find a profitable market. Paper-mills and flour mills might be established in greater numbers. There are openings also for the manufacture of sewing machines, fire-works, rope, boots and shoes, saddlery, harness, clocks, watches, aniline and alazarine dyes, electrical appliances, glass and glassware, tea chests, gloves, rice, starch, matches, lamps, candles, soap, linen, hardware and cutlery.

Obviously, India might be largely self-sufficing, and, as of old, export her surplus. But now her imports are rising, and under the present system her exports do not enrich her as they should.

Imports were steadily rising before the War, but dropped with it (amounts given in pounds sterling):

1911-12 —	92,383,200	Piece Goods	28,592,000
12-13 —	107,332,490	—	35,536,000
13-14 —	122,165,203	—	38,758,000
14-15 —	91,952,600	—	28,643,000
15-16 —	87,560,169	—	25,175,000

The previous five years also show generally rising imports (amounts given in rupees):

1906-7	—	135,50,85,676
7-8	—	162,71,55,234
8-9	—	143,89,75,796
9-10	—	154,48,36,214
10-11	—	169,05,72,729

Exports exceeded imports, and the War has made difficulties in the way of realising payment. (Amounts given in pounds sterling.)

1911-12	—	147,879,060
12-13	—	160,899,289
13-14	—	162,807,900
14-15	—	118,323,300
15-16	—	128,356,619

Indian merchants have seen the swift expansion of Japanese trade, and know that it is fostered by the Japanese Government both by protection and with bounties. They have to compete with it in their own land. Is it any wonder that they desire an Indian Government? They see Japanese goods underselling them and flooding their own markets.

Is it any wonder that they desire a Home Government, that will put duties on these foreign goods and protect their own products?

The furious uprising of the European Associations, ever indifferent to politics which only concern Indian interests, has shown them that their trade rivals dread the transfer of power, because they fear to lose the unfair privileges and advantages which they have always enjoyed, since the humble traders of the seventeenth century became the masters of India. They are not accustomed to a struggle on equal terms, and the prospect dismays them. They want privilege, not justice and a fair field. Much of their fear and anger, the need felt by Sir Hugh Bray for English dominance for the protection of English interests, lie in the fact that they dread the Budget of a Home Government, even more than they dread a fair trade competition.

The Indian merchants now realise that in the trade-war after the end of the present War, they will go down, unless they have power in their own country. Trade, commerce, industry, organised by the countrymen of the European Chambers of Commerce and Trade Associations, mean ruin to the Indian merchants, traders and manufacturers. The favouritism of Governments and English Banks has spelt hard struggle during the period when organisation was wanting. When it is accompanied by organisation created and ruled by the foreigners, it will spell ruin. Mr. J. W. Root has rightly observed that to give Great Britain, under present circumstances,

> the control over Indian foreign trade and internal industry that would be secured by a common tariff would be an unpardonable iniquity. . . Can it be conceived that were India's fiscal arrangements placed to any considerable extent under the control of British legislators, they would not be regulated with an eye to British interests? Intense jealousy

of India is always cropping up in everything affecting fiscal or industrial legislation.

Indian merchants are fully alive to this danger, and to avert it they are welcoming Home Rule.

The merchants also realise that fiscal autonomy can only come with political autonomy. Only the illogical demand fiscal autonomy and reject Home Rule. A budget framed by an Indian Finance Member would aim at a much increased expenditure on education, sanitation and irrigation—an expenditure that would result in increased capacity and increased health for the citizens and increased productiveness for the land. Railways would be constructed out of loans raised for the particular project, not out of revenue. Administration charges would be reduced by the reduction of salaries and greater economy. They have increased in a decade by Rs. 160 millions.

On the revenue side, the taxation on land would be lightened, so that cultivators might make a decent living by their labour. Exports of Indian monopolies, such as jute and indigo, would be heavily taxed. Imports would be taxed according to India's needs, and heavy duties laid on bounty-fed products. Imported liquors would carry a prohibitory duty, and they were imported in 1910-11 to the value of Rs. 1,89,81,666. Provisions, which were imported to the value of over 3 crores of rupees, might also be heavily taxed, being a luxury. Sugar rose in five years from 10 crores of rupees to 14 crores, and should be heavily taxed, so as to encourage its growth here. Cotton piece-goods have risen from 37 crores to 41 crores and India should supply herself, as well as with silk piece-goods, risen from $1\frac{3}{4}$ crores to $2\frac{3}{4}$ crores. Army expenditure at the moment cannot be reduced, but later, Territorial Armies would be raised and large reserves gradually formed. For a time English troops would remain, as in the South African Union, but the short service system would be abolished, and recruiting charges reduced.

Even so hasty a glance over the economic condition of India makes very plain the reasons for the awakening of Indian Merchants, and their entry into the Home Rule Camp.

(*e*) *The Awakening of the Women*

The position of women in the ancient Āryan civilisation was a very noble one. The great majority married, becoming, as Manu said, the Light of the Home; some took up the ascetic life, remained unmarried, and sought the knowledge of Brahman. The story of the Rāṇī Ḍamayanṭī, to whom her husband's Ministers came, when they were troubled by the Rājā's gambling; that of Gānḍhārī, in the Council of Kings and warrior Chiefs, remonstrating with her headstrong son; in later days, those of Paḍmāvaṭī of Chittoor, of Mīrābai of Mārwār, the sweet poetess, of Tārābai of Ṭhoḍa, the warrior, of Chānd Bibi, the defender of Ahmeḍnagar, of Ahālaya Bai of Indore, the great ruler—all these and countless others are well known.

Only in the last five or six generations have the Indian women slipped away from their place at their husbands' side, and left them unhelped in public life. Even now, they wield great influence over husband and son, but lack thorough knowledge to aid. Culture has never forsaken them, but the English education of their husbands and sons, with the neglect of Saṁskṛṭ and the Vernacular, have made a barrier between the culture of the husband and that of the wife, and have shut the woman out from her old sympathy with the larger life of men. While the interests of the husband have widened, those of the wife have narrowed. The materialising of the husband has tended also, by re-action, to render the wife's religion less broad and wise, and by throwing her on the family priest for guidance in religion, instead, as of old, on her husband, has made the religion entirely one of devotion; and lacking the strong stimulus of knowledge, it more easily slides down into superstition, into dependence on forms not understood.

The wish to save their sons from the materialising results of English education awoke keen sympathy among Indian mothers with the movement to make Hinḍūism an integral part of education. It was, perhaps, the first movement in modern days which aroused among them in all parts of India a keen and living interest.

Then the troubles of Indians outside India roused the ever-quick sympathy of Indian women, and the attack in South Africa on the sacredness of Indian marriage drew large numbers of them out of their homes to protest against the wrong.

The Partition of Bengal was bitterly resented by Beṅgāli women, and was another factor in the outward-turning change. When the editor of an Extremist newspaper was prosecuted for sedition, convicted and sentenced, 500 Beṅgāli women went to his mother to show their sympathy, not by condolences, but by congratulations. Such was the feeling of the well-born women of Bengal.

The Indentured Labour question, involving the dishonour of women, again, moved them deeply, and even sent a deputation to the Viceroy composed of women.

These were, perhaps, the chief outer causes; but deep in the heart of India's daughters arose the Mother's voice, calling on them to help her to arise, and to be once more mistress in her own household. Indian women, nursed on her old literature, with its wonderful ideals of womanly perfection, could not remain indifferent to the great movement for India's liberty. And during the last few years the hidden fire long burning in their hearts, fire of love to Bhāraṭamāṭā, fire of resentment against the lessened influence of the religion which they passionately love, instinctive dislike of the foreigner as ruling in their land, have caused a marvellous awakening. The strength of the Home Rule movement is rendered tenfold greater by the adhesion to it of large numbers of women, who bring to its helping the uncalculating heroism, the endurance, the self-sacrifice, of the feminine nature. Our League's best recruits and recruiters are among the women of India, and the women of Madras boast that they marched in procession when the men were stopped, and that their prayers in the temples set the interned captives free. Home Rule has become so intertwined with religion by the prayers offered up in the great southern Temples—sacred places of pilgrimage—and spreading from them to village temples, and also by its being preached, up and down the country, by Sāḍhus and Sannyāsins, that it has become in the minds of the women and of the ever-religious masses, inextricably intertwined with religion. That is, in this country, the surest way of winning alike the women of the higher classes and the men and women villagers. And that is why I just said that the two words, "Home Rule," have become a Manṭram.

(*f*) *The Awakening of the Masses*

This is another startling phenomenon of our times, due of late to the teaching of Sāḍhus and Sannyāsins and the campaign of prayer, just mentioned, but much more to the steady influence of the educated classes permeating the masses for very many years, the classes which, as we shall see, have their roots struck deep in the villages. It must be remembered that the raiyaṭ, though innocent of English, has a culture of his own, made up of old traditions and legends and folk-lore, coming down from time immemorial. He is religious, knows the great laws of Karma and Reincarnation, is industrious and shrewd. He cares very little for who is the "Sirkar," and very much for the agents who come to collect his tax, or to meddle with his fields. In the old days, which, for him still live, the Pañchāyaṭ managed the village affairs, and he was prosperous and contented, save when the King's tax-gatherer came, or soldiers harried his village. These were inevitable natural evils, like drought or flood; and if a raid came or an invasion, they felt they were suffering with their King, as in the tax they were sharing with their King, whereas they are crushed now in an iron machinery, without the human nexus that used to exist.

Home Rule has touched the raiyat through his village life, where the present order presses hardly upon him in ways that I shall refer to when dealing with agricultural conditions. He resents the rigid payment of tax in money instead of the variable tax in kind, the King's share of the produce. He resents the frequent resettlements, which force him to borrow from the money-lender to meet the higher claim. He wants the old Pañchāyaṭ back again ; he wants that his village should be managed by himself and his fellows, and he wants to get rid of the tyranny of petty officials, who have replaced the old useful communal servants.

We cannot leave out of the causes which have helped to awaken the masses, the influence of the Co-operative Movement, and the visits paid to villages by educated men for lectures on sanitation, hygiene, and other subjects. Messrs. Moreland and Ewing writing in the *Quarterly Review*, remarked:

> The change of attitude on the part of the peasant, coupled with the progress made in organisation mainly through the Co-operative propaganda, is the outstanding achievement of the past decade, and at the same time the chief ground for the recent confidence with which agricultural reformers can now face the future.

In many parts of the country, where Conferences are carried on in the vernacular, the raiyats attend in large numbers, and often take part in the practical discussions on local affairs. They have begun to hope, and to feel that they are a part of the great National Movement, and that for them also a better day is dawning.

The submerged classes have also felt the touch of a ray of hope, and are lifting up their bowed heads, and claiming, with more and more definiteness, their place in the Household of the Mother. Movements, created by themselves, or originating in the higher castes, have been stirring in them a sense of self-respect. The Brāhmaṇas, awakening to a sense of their long-neglected duty, have done much to help them, and the prospect of their future brightens year by year.

By a just karma the higher castes are finding that attempts are being made by official and non-official Europeans to stir this class into opposition to Home Rule. They play upon the contempt with which they had been treated, and threaten them with a return of it, if "Brāhmaṇa Rule," as they call it, is gained. Twenty years ago and more, I ventured to urge the danger to Hindu Society that was hidden within the neglect of the submerged, and the folly of making it profitable for them to embrace Islām or Christianity, which offered them a higher social status. Much has been done since then, but it is only a drop in the ocean needed. They know very well, of course, that all the castes, not the highest alone, are equally guilty, but that is a sorry comfort. Large numbers of them are, happily, willing to forget the past, and to work with their Indian fellow-countrymen for the future. It is the urgent duty of every lover of the Motherland to draw these, her neglected children, into the common Home.

Mr. Gandhi's capital idea of a monster petition for the Congress-League Scheme, for which signatures were only to be taken after careful explanation of its scope and meaning, has proved to be an admirable method of political propaganda. The soil in the Madras Presidency had been well prepared by a wide distribution of popular literature, and the Propaganda Committee had scattered over the land in the vernaculars a simple explanation of Home Rule. The result of active work in the villages during the last year showed itself in the gathering in less than a month of nearly a million signatures. They have been taken in duplicate, so that we have a record of a huge number of people, interested in Home Rule, and the hosts will increase in ever widening circles, preparing for the coming Freedom.

WHY INDIA DEMANDS HOME RULE

India demands Home Rule for two reasons, one essential and vital, the other less important but weighty: First, because Freedom is the birthright of every Nation; secondly, because her most important interests are now made subservient to the interests of the British Empire without her consent, and her resources are not utilised for her greatest needs. It is enough only to mention the money spent on her Army, not for local defence but for Imperial purposes, as compared with that spent on primary Education.

I. The Vital Reason

(a) *What is a Nation?*

Self-Government is necessary to the self-respect and dignity of a People ; Other-Government emasculates a Nation, lowers its character, and lessons its capacity. The wrong done by the Arms Act, which Rājā Rāmpāl Singh voiced in the Second Congress as a wrong which outweighed all the benefits of British Rule, was its weakening and debasing effect on Indian manhood. "We cannot," he declared, "be grateful to it for degrading our natures, for systematically crushing out all martial spirit, for converting a race of soldiers and heroes into a timid flock of quill-driving sheep." This was done not by the fact that a man did not carry arms—few carry them in England—but that men were deprived of the *right* to carry them. A Nation, an individual, cannot develop his capacities to the utmost without Liberty. And this is recognised everywhere except in India. As Mazzini truly said:

> God has written a line of His thought over the cradle of every people. That is its special mission. It cannot be cancelled; it must be freely developed.

For what is a Nation? It is a spark of the Divine Fire, a fragment of the Divine Life, outbreathed into the world, and gathering round itself a mass of individuals, men, women and children, whom it binds together into one. Its qualities, its powers, in a word, its type, depend on the fragment of the Divine Life embodied in it, the Life which shapes it, evolves it, colours it and makes it One. The magic of Nationality is the feeling of oneness, and the use of Nationality is to serve the world in the particular way for which its type fits it. This is what Mazzini called "its special mission," the duty given to it by God in its birth-hour. Thus India had the duty of spreading the idea of Ḍharma, Persia that of Purity, Egypt that of Science, Greece that of Beauty, Rome that of Law. But to render its full service to Humanity it must develop along its own lines, and be Self-determined in its evolution. It must be Itself, and not Another. The whole world suffers where a Nationality is distorted or suppressed, before its mission to the world is accomplished.

(*b*) *The Cry for Self-Rule*

Hence the cry of a Nation for Freedom, for Self-Rule, is not a cry of mere selfishness, demanding more Rights that it may enjoy more happiness. Even in that there is nothing wrong, for happiness means fulness of life, and to enjoy such fulness is a righteous claim. But the demand for Self-Rule is a demand for the evolution of its own nature for the Service of Humanity. It is a demand of the deepest Spirituality, an expression of the longing to give its very best to the world. Hence dangers cannot check it, nor threats appal, nor offerings of greater pleasures lure it to give up its demand for Freedom. In the adapted words of a Christian Scripture, it passionately cries: "What shall it profit a Nation if it gain the whole world and lose its own Soul? What shall a Nation give in exchange for its Soul?" Better hardship and freedom, than luxury and thraldom. This is the spirit of the Home Rule movement, and therefore it cannot be crushed, it cannot be destroyed, it is eternal and ever young. Nor can it be persuaded to exchange its birthright for any mess of efficiency-pottage at the hands of the bureaucracy.

(c) *Stunting the Race*

Coming closer to the daily life of the people as individuals, we see that the character of each man, woman and child is degraded and weakened by a foreign administration, and this is most keenly felt by the best Indians. Speaking on the employment of Indians in the Public Services, Gopāl Kṛshṇa Gokhale said:

> A kind of dwarfing or stunting of the Indian race is going on under the present system. We must live all the days of our life in an atmosphere of inferiority, and the tallest of us must bend, in order that the exigencies of the system may be satisfied. The upward impulse, if I may use such an expression, which every schoolboy at Eton or Harrow may feel, that he may one day be a Gladstone, a Nelson, or a Wellington, and which may draw forth the best efforts of which he is capable, that is denied to us. The full height to which our manhood is capable of rising can never be reached by us under the present system. The moral elevation which every Self-governing people feel cannot be felt by us. Our administrative and military talents must gradually disappear owing to sheer disuse, till at last our lot, as hewers of wood and drawers of water in our own country, is stereotyped.

The Hon. Mr. Bhupendranath Basu has spoken on similar lines:

> A bureaucratic administration, conducted by an imported agency, and centering all power in its

hands, and undertaking all responsibility, has acted as a dead weight on the Soul of India, stifling in us all sense of initiative, for the lack of which we are condemned, atrophying the nerves of action, and, what is most serious, necessarily dwarfing in us all feeling of self-respect.

In this connection the warning of Lord Salisbury to Cooper's Hill students is significant:

> No system of Government can be permanently safe where there is a feeling of inferiority or of mortification affecting the relations between the governing and the governed. There is nothing I would more earnestly wish to impress upon all who leave this country for the purpose of governing India than that, if they choose to be so, they are the only enemies England has to fear. They are the persons who can, if they will, deal a blow of the deadliest character at the future rule of England.

I have ventured to urge this danger, which has increased of late years, in consequence of the growing self-respect of the Indians. But the ostrich policy is thought to be preferable in my part of the country.

This stunting of the race begins with the education of the child. The Schools differentiate between British and Indian teachers; the Colleges do the same. The students see first-class Indians superseded by young and third-rate foreigners; the Principal of a College should be a foreigner; foreign history is more important than Indian; to have written on English villages is a qualification for teaching economics in India; the whole atmosphere of the School and the College emphasises the superiority of the foreigner, even when the professors abstain from open assertion thereof. The Education Department controls the education given, and it is planned on foreign models, and its object is to serve foreign rather than native ends, to make docile Government servants rather than patriotic citizens; high spirits, courage, self-respect, are not encouraged, and docility is regarded as the most precious quality in the student; pride in country, patriotism, ambition, are looked on as dangerous, and English, instead of Indian, Ideals are exalted; the blessings of a foreign rule and the incapacity of Indians to manage their own affairs are constantly inculcated. What wonder that boys thus trained often turn out, as men, time-servers and sycophants, and, finding their legitimate ambitions frustrated, become selfish and care little for the public weal? Their own inferiority has been so driven into them during their most impressionable years, that they do not even feel what Mr. Asquith called the "intolerable degradation of a foreign yoke".

(*d*) *India's Rights*

It is not a question whether the rule is good or bad. German efficiency in Germany is far greater than English efficiency in England; the Germans were better fed, had more amusements and leisure, less crushing poverty than the English. But would any Englishman therefore desire to see Germans occupying all the highest positions in England? Why not? Because the righteous self-respect and dignity of the free man revolt against foreign domination, however superior. As Mr. Asquith said at the beginning of the War, such a condition was "inconceivable and would be intolerable". Why then is it the one conceivable system here in India? Why is it not felt by all Indians to be intolerable? It is because it has become a habit, bred in us from childhood, to regard the Sāhab-log as our natural superiors, and the greatest injury British rule has done to Indians is to deprive them of the natural instinct born in all free peoples, the feeling of an inherent right to Self-determination, to be themselves. Indian dress, Indian food, Indian ways, Indian customs, are all looked on as second-rate;

Indian mother-tongue and Indian literature cannot make an educated man. Indians as well as Englishmen take it for granted that the natural rights of every Nation do not belong to them; they claim "a larger share in the Government of the country," instead of claiming the Government of their own country, and they are expected to feel grateful for "boons," for concessions. Britain is to say what she will give. The whole thing is wrong, topsy-turvy, irrational. Thank God that India's eyes are opening; that myriads of her people realise that they are men, with a man's right to freedom in his own country, a man's right to manage his own affairs. India is no longer on her knees for boons; she is on her feet for Rights. It is because I have taught this, that the English in India misunderstand me, and call me seditious; it is because I have taught this, that I am President of this Congress to-day.

This may seem strong language, because the plain truth is not usually put in India. But this is what every Briton feels in Britain for his own country, and what every Indian should feel in India for his. This is the Freedom for which the Allies are fighting; this is Democracy, the Spirit of the Age. And this is what every true Briton will feel is India's Right, the moment India claims it for herself, as she is claiming it now. When this Right is gained, then will the tie between India and Great Britain become a golden link of mutual love and service, and the iron chain of a foreign yoke will fall away. We shall live and work side by side, with no sense of distrust and dislike, working as brothers for common ends. And from that union shall arise the mightiest Empire, or rather Commonwealth, that the world has ever known, a Commonwealth that, in God's good time, shall put an end to War.

II. The Secondary Reasons

(a) *Tests of Efficiency*

The Secondary Reason for the present demand for Home Rule may be summed up in the blunt statement: "The present rule, while efficient in less important matters and in those which concern British interest, is inefficient in the greater matters on which the healthy life and happiness of the people depend." Looking at outer things, such as external order, posts and telegraphs—except where political agitators are concerned—main roads, railways, etc., foreign visitors, who expected to find a semi-savage country, hold up their hands in admiration. But if they saw the life of the people, the masses of struggling clerks trying to educate their children on Rs. 25 (33s. 4d.) a month, the masses of labourers with one meal a day, and the huts in which they live, they would find cause for thought. And if the educated men talked freely with them, they would be surprised at their bitterness. Gopāl Kṛṣhṇa Gokhale put the whole matter very plainly in 1911:

> One of the fundamental conditions of the peculiar position of the British Government in this country is that it should be a continuously progressive Government. I think all thinking men, to whatever community they belong, will accept that. Now, I suggest four tests to judge whether the Government is progressive, and further whether it is continuously progressive. The first test that I would apply is: What measures it adopts for the moral and material improvement of the mass of the people, and under these measures I do not include those appliances of modern Governments which the British Government has applied in this country, because they were appliances necessary for its very existence, though they have benefited the people, such as the construction of Railways, the introduction of Post and Telegraphs, and things of that kind. By measures for the moral and material improvement of the people, I mean what the Government does for Education, what the Government does for Sanitation, what the Government does for Agricultural development, and so forth. That is my

first test. The second test that I would apply is: What steps the Government takes to give us a larger share in the administration of our local affairs—in municipalities and local boards. My third test is: What voice the Government gives us in its Councils —in those deliberative assemblies, where policies are considered. And, lastly, we must consider how far Indians are admitted into the ranks of the Public Service.

[*Here ends the reprint*]

On all these tests, Mr. Gokhale points out the British Government has definitely failed! But we cannot afford the space to follow out that matter here.

CHAPTER VI

THE STRUGGLE OVER THE REFORMS

DEATH OF THE OLD CONGRESS
THE REFORMED LEGISLATURES

IT will be but right to remark at this point that the most statesmanlike action on the part of Great Britain would have been to realise that the educated classes of India were, at this time, heartily at one as to the vital necessity of preserving the British connection and remaining within the Empire. Having held up before India the Ideal of Responsible Government—which, be it remembered, was not found in the Congress-League Scheme—it would have been better to have boldly abandoned autocracy in theory, and in practice to have introduced complete responsibility, except for law and order, at least in the Provincial Governments, even if only partial responsibility was given in the Central. There was much eagerness in the country, but a very friendly spirit predominated in the early part of 1918, and a willingness to work Reforms which were less than the people desired.

Unhappily at this very time a furious agitation against the proposed Reforms was going on in England, led by Lord Sydenham and other reactionaries. An Indo-British Association had been formed, and every means known to the English politician was used against Indian freedom. The bureaucracy in India rallied against the dreaded Reforms, and in both countries the one effort made was to minimise them; pressure was put on Mr. Montagu, proposals were made to forbid discussion in India, and when the Home Rule Leagues sought to counter all this by sending Deputations to England, the first leaving India in the middle of March, 1918, the passports of the delegates were cancelled by the War Cabinet, they were landed at Gibraltar, and detained there for six weeks. This arbitrary conduct gave rise to some anger in India, but until April, educative work went on quietly. Then the National Party began to show signs of division in Madras, and this came to a head in the Provincial Conference in May, where a bitter attack was made on myself and others as being willing to accept inadequate Reforms, and a note was struck which sounded again at Amritsar in 1919, and was repeated at Calcutta in September, 1920—"Boycott the Councils".

Mr. Tilak, indeed, and myself were blamed because he had said, and I agreed with him, that he would utilise to the utmost even a fragment of reform, in order to get the whole. Much discussion went on in the early months of 1918 as to the forthcoming Reforms, some proposing to stay out of the new Councils if the Reforms were inadequate, while we said we should go into them and utilise all they gave in order to reach our goal (*Commonweal*, May 24, 1918, p. 294). A week after, returning to the subject, I urged that we should agitate for all we wanted, but "that if the inadequate Reforms are, despite the agitation, embodied in a statute, the country will not boycott the new Councils, but will utilise them to win Home Rule" (*Ibid.*, May 31, p. 310). In the light of subsequent events the following words seem almost prophetic:

> It has been asked me in private conversation: Why raise that question now, before the statute is passed? Because if, in a natural surge of anger and distrust, on finding the Reforms to be inadequate, persons committed themselves to the policy of boycotting the new Councils, it might be difficult for them to retrace their steps, and Parliament,

relieved from the fear of an "Irish" party in the new Councils, that would prove a continual difficulty, would ignore the agitation and sit tight, and pass their inadequate measure. There is such a thing as foresight in political work, and it may sometimes be well to look ahead. (*Ibid.*)

How the wrath originated and gathered will be told in the next chapter; meanwhile the outline of the Reform Act story may be finished here. The Reform proposals came out as the *Montagu-Chelmsford Report* in July, 1918. They were probably the best that could be secured in the midst of the contending parties, putting tremendous pressure on Mr. Montagu. Three attitudes were taken up in India: the "Moderates" accepted them, but asked for considerable alterations; the "Home Rulers" did not accept them, but urged similar modifications which would suffice for the time; the "Extremists" declined to accept them at all. A Special Congress, held in Bombay on August 29 to September 1, was attended in force by the two last-named parties, and by a considerable number of the first, and a compromise was arrived at which, declaring the Reforms to be "inadequate, unsatisfactory and disappointing," yet agreed on resolutions which would widen them and make them workable. The Moderates held their separate Conference in October, and made very similar amendments, but added no condemnatory words. At the Delhi Congress at Christmas, 1918, this pact was broken by the Extremists, against the protest of the Home Rulers and two or three Moderates, and the breach between these and the Extremists was completed. Two separate Deputations went in 1919 from the Congress and the Moderate Conference, and two from the Home Rule Leagues. For, in February, 1919, the All-India Home Rule League split in twain, when I opposed Mr. Gandhi's proposal of starting "passive resistance" against the Rowlatt Act; the Bombay and Madras Councils united to oust me from the Presidency, while a large party elected me as the President of the other section, which took the name of the National Home Rule League. Each sent a deputation to England and both did very useful work, collaborating with each other and with the Moderates, and obtaining large amendments in the Reform Bill. This came, as an Act, before the Amritsar Congress of 1919, and there the split became final. I stood for the Reform Act with a small band of 30 National Home Rulers against the Congress resolution denouncing the Act in the language of 1918, despite the radical changes in it which had been made. The older League stood by Mr. M. K. Gandhi, and it finally succumbed entirely to his influence, changed its constitution, and became the Swarāj League, part of the Non-Co-Operation movement. The National Home Rule League worked for the Reform Act, sending out immense numbers of explanatory leaflets in English and in the leading vernaculars, and co-operated with the "Moderates," who took the name of "Liberals," both opposing the Non-Co-Operation movement, as will be shown later, and supporting each other's candidates in the elections of 1920.

In 1920, the Congress at Nāgpūr, at the instance of Mr. M. K. Gandhi, adopted a new Constitution, presented by a Committee of which he was Chairman, changed its objective —Self-Government "on Colonial lines," *i.e.*, within the British Empire—to Swarāj, Self-Government, pure and simple, thus leaving open the question of "within or without," and making legitimate a motion for Indian Independence, such as was proposed at the Ahmedabad Congress in 1921. The motion there was rejected, but it was proved that at Nāgpūr had come the final parting of the ways, one leading to the realisation of the original dream, India as a Free Nation in a world-wide Federation of Free Nations, the greatest World-Power; the other leading to her Independence as a solitary Nation. Thus has arisen the problem with which we are now faced as to "The Future of Indian Politics".

The words that "ultimate freedom under her [Britain's] rule was inevitable," are being proved true under our eyes to-day. The question as to "The Future of Indian Politics" in 1922—seven years after the above words were printed—is no longer whether India shall be free, shall have Self-Government, but: "What shall be the nature of that Self-Government? Shall India claim Independence, stepping outside the Empire, or shall she be a Free Nation in a Commonwealth of Free Nations? Shall the connection between India and Britain be maintained, as valuable and beneficial to both, or shall it be rent in twain?"

This question had not arisen as a question in practical politics before 1920, and then only by implication. It had been talked of by a handful of educated men, driven to despair by the policy of Lord Curzon, while Viceroy of India. His arrogance, his arbitrary methods, his high-handed disregard of Indian feeling, his evident wish to stem the rising tide of National political activity, had roused sentiments of antagonism, of outraged self-respect, of determined resistance, and had inflamed hundreds of high-spirited and passionate youths to a madness of rebellion. Lord Minto was sent to India to pour oil on the troubled waters, and the Minto-Morley Reforms were evolved, vitiated by the view of the then Secretary of State that India was not, and was not likely to come, within sight of Parliamentary institutions. The Reformed Councils were given a *minority* of elected members, and proved to be useless both for legislation and as training grounds for future legislators. They gave neither power nor responsibility; their first measure in the Central Council, Act 1 of 1910, was the Press Act, against which all the efforts, made by a gallant few, came to naught. Over and over again, the members struggled in vain against evil measures; in Madras they could not even abolish the stocks in villages, used for low-class offenders, and the Councils were indignantly described by a member in a final session as "a farce". In the Central Council, despite the desperate resistance of the elected members, was passed the infamous Rowlatt Act, the agitation against which began the Non-Co-Operation Movement, the Hon. Paṇḍiṭ Maḍan Mohan Malaviya was left to battle alone in his effort to bring the Panjāb atrocities to public notice, and in the last Session came the refusal of the Viceroy—in answer to the Hon. Mr. V. S. Srinivasa Sastri's request—to give a day for the discussion of that same Panjāb tragedy. The "official bloc" as it was called, was the "machinery of autocracy" in the Central Legislative Council.

The Reform Act of 1919 gave a large elected *majority* of members in the Central Assembly and the Provincial Councils, and a working *majority* in the Council of State. The Executive Government in the Provinces was formed of an Executive Council of two or four Councillors, half Indian and half British, irremovable, and responsible only to the Governor, dealing with certain subjects called "reserved," and two or three Ministers, all Indian, representing the majority in the Council and responsible to it, dealing with subjects styled "transferred". In the Central Government there was the Viceroy's Executive Council of three Indians and three British, responsible to the Viceroy only. But a majority of elected members and an irresponsible Council cannot long co-exist. Surely, and with unexpected rapidity, power is passing into the hands of the Legislature. A Government must carry its Legislature with it, or must provoke hopeless deadlocks, which, as experience in the Colonies has proved, bring about ere long Responsible Government. And India is well on the way to Dominion status. "Ultimate Freedom under Britain's rule is inevitable," and is almost within her grasp.

The first elections under the Reform Act took place in the autumn of 1920. The Non-Co-Operation movement (see below in Chapter VII) was then in full swing, and in the Calcutta Special Congress of that year, meeting on September 1, the boycott of the New Councils was carried after a hot discussion and tumultuous uproar. It was so far successful as to shut out many capable and well-known men, who preferred obedience to the "Congress mandate" to the openings for constitutional advance offered under the Reform Act. The elections were marked by great bitterness, and much intimidation from those who were working to nullify the Reform Act, preferring "direct action" to Parliamentary procedure. On the one side were many honoured leaders, who while expressing dislike of the mandate yet thought that loyalty to the Nation demanded obedience to the Congress; on the other side were practically all the old leaders of the great days of Congress struggle, with the advanced Liberals and the National Home Rulers, united in one opposition to the Non-Co-Operation movement, and in determination to work to their utmost the Reforms for which they had fought so long, believing that loyalty to the Nation demanded disobedience to the Congress. On both sides were patriots, thinking only of their country's good, and cruel were the separations brought about by opposing views in those who for long had worked together; heart-rending was the breaking of the tie with the Congress, but for the first time obedience to its mandate was demanded from a dissident minority. Until then the Congress had been free, open to all who were ready to work for freedom within the Empire: in 1915, it had, as already related, made easy the return of those who had left it in 1907 and had not already returned. But in 1920, it had adopted Non-Co-Operation, and the new Constitution, to be adopted at Nàgpūr, shut out of its organisation those who stood against the tyranny of a majority, and rejected "direct action". The old free Congress was dead, and the loss to those who had built it was in verity heart-rending.

The elections returned, despite all terrorism, —even physical exclusion from the polling booths—Liberals and Home Rulers, with a sprinkling of Conservatives, sent by special classes. The Provincial Councils and the

Central Legislature—consisting of the Legislative Assembly and the Council of State, elected on different registers—opened at the beginning of 1921.

H.R.H. the Duke of Connaught came to open the four chief Legislatures, and landing on January 10, opened the Madras Council on January 12. The Bengal Council he opened on February 3. On February 9, he opened the Council of State and the Indian Legislative Assembly in Delhi. Then was autocracy declared both by Viceroy and Duke to be abandoned. Then did the King send his message, proclaiming "the beginning of Swarāj within my Empire". Then did King and Duke speak of their sorrow for the Panjāb tragedy and their sympathy with the sufferers. The Duke's words, broken by strong emotion, moved the whole great assembly and have rung round India. Their effect has been seen in the co-operation they created. The Bombay Council was opened by H.R.H. on February 23. Then the Royal Messenger of Peace and Goodwill went home, his work accomplished.

The new spirit of co-operation showed itself at once. The Council of State held its first Government business day on February 14, and the Government gave place to the Hon.

Mr. V. S. Srinivasa Sastri, who moved a resolution, accepted by the Government, to examine the Repressive Laws on the Statute Book and report on their repeal or amendment. The "Repressive Laws" are those which substitute Executive for Judicial action, and since 1804 have been used arbitrarily to repress political efforts for Reform, placing liberty and property at the mercy of the Executive. In the Assembly, following up this resolution, Mr. O'Donnell moved and carried a resolution for a Committee to examine and report on the Press Laws. Two Committees were consequently appointed, one to deal with Political Offences, the other with Acts affecting the Press. The first was composed of seven Indians and two Englishmen, the second of eight Indians and one Englishman, and both were presided over by the Indian Law Member of the Viceroy's Executive Council, the Hon. Dr. Tej Bahāḍūr Sapru.

The Laws submitted to the first Committee were:

The Bengal State Offences Regulation, 1804, Madras Regulation 7 of 1808, Bengal State Prisoners Regulation, 1818, Madras Regulation 2 of 1819, Bombay Regulation 25 of 1827, State Prisoners Act, 1850, State Offences Act, 1857, Forfeiture Act, 1857, State Prisoners Act, 1858, Indian Criminal Law Amendment Act, 1908, Prevention of Seditious Meetings Act, 1911, Defence of India Act, 1915, Criminal Law Amendment Act, 1915, and Anarchical and Revolutionary Crimes Act, 1919 (the Rowlatt Act).

The Press Laws were:

The Press and Registration Books Act 1867, Indian Press Act, 1910, and Newspaper (Incitement to Offences) Act, 1900.

The Committees, after taking written and oral evidence, both reported unanimously in favour of the repeal of the whole of these Acts, except the Registration Act of 1867, a necessary law, which was only slightly amended. The first Committee recommended that the Seditious Meetings Act, 1911, and the second Part of the Criminal Law Amendment

Act, 1911 (penalising unlawful associations) should be repealed when the country was less disturbed, but that the whole of the rest should be repealed at once. The Reports were accepted. Repealing Bills were introduced, carried, and approved by the Viceroy. Thus disappeared the legislation which had been used to penalise even constitutional proposals of Reform, and had caused furious antagonism and an unspeakable amount of misery; this was done at a time when the revolutionary Non-Co-Operation Movement (1922) was trying to overthrow and destroy the Government, and it is a striking proof of the sincerity of their determination to work in the spirit of the Reforms, that, at this critical moment, they laid down their most effective weapons.

The Government gave the first working day in the Legislative Assembly to a resolution moved by Mr. Jamnāḍās Ḍwārkaḍās and accepted by the Government, that expressed regret for the unnecessary humiliations and hardships inflicted on Indians in the Panjāb tragedy, asserted the equality of Indians and Europeans in the sanctity of life and honour, stated some of the punishments inflicted on guilty officers, and promised liberal compensation to families who had suffered in the Jallianwalla Bagh massacre, on a scale similar to that awarded to the British victims. General Dyer had been removed from the Indian Army—"a disgrace worse than death," the action was called by a brother officer. Sir Michael O'Dwyer, who had goaded the Province into hatred of the British Government, had retired, and was out of reach. Here again the whole spirit was changed, sympathy and regret had taken the place of cruel hatred and contempt; 1,700 condemned prisoners were released out of 1,786; a political reformer who had been condemned to an extravagant sentence of transportation and confiscation is now an honoured Minister in the Panjāb; the administration of Martial Law was reformed, so that no such excesses could happen again, as was proved during the Malabar Rebellion in 1921, 1922.

It would take too long even to run over the useful work done; Both in 1921 and 1922, the Indian and Provincial Legislatures have sweepingly reduced the Budgets; in March, 1922, the Assembly refused 9½ crores of additional taxation—a crore is rupees ten million—and reduced the expenses nearly another crore, and its decisions have been accepted. In the Provinces great reductions have also been made. The Assembly has asserted fiscal autonomy, both in its first and second years, taking the tariff into its own hands; and Mr. Montagu, the Secretary of State for India, has justified its action and has declared that interference would be a taking away of what had been given. Woman Suffrage has been gained in two Provinces, and the Assembly has given its franchise to all women on Provincial registers. When an impudent member of Parliament complained that a "convicted rebel" has been made a Minister, the Speaker of the House of Commons told him that "the House of Commons had given practical Home Rule, or something akin to Home Rule, to the Councils, and the less it interfered with the Councils the better". A Factory Act has been passed, improving the conditions of Labour, and another giving registration to Trade Unions. Territorial Armies are being trained, and an "Indian Sandhurst" has been opened for the training of Indian officers. Simultaneous examinations are held in India and England for the Civil Service. Executive and Judicial functions have been separated in several Provinces. A Committee is sitting to report on the removal of racial distinctions in legal procedure. A Fiscal Commission has travelled over India, taking evidence, and is now considering its Report. In a disagreement that arose between the Bengal Council and the Governor, the latter made the remarkable declaration that if there arose an "unbridgeable cleavage of opinion extending over the administrative field, between the Governor and the Council," then

> the Governor himself would realise that his usefulness either to the Government or the Province had come to an end, and he would be justified in demanding release from responsibilities which he was no longer able satisfactorily to discharge. If things so turned out that such a situation did become applicable in my own case, I should accept it in good part.

When it is remembered that in 1919 the Governors were autocrats, presiding over Legislative Chambers with elected members in a perpetual minority, such a speech in 1921 may be admitted to prove a startling change, and to prove also the folly of those who boycotted the Councils, and preferred the way of "direct action," which has only led to misery and bloodshed, as we shall see in the next chapter, without bringing about one of the desired changes.[1]

Nor must other changes be forgotten, altering the status of India. Sir Saṭyenḍra Sinha was made Under-Secretary of State for India, and was later made a Peer, to represent her in the House of Lords. The Government of India nominated Indians to the Imperial Council, two of them being raised to the rank of Privy Councillors. The Rt. Hon. V. S. Srinivāsa Sāsṭri succeeded in passing there a resolution, agreed to by all except the representative of South Africa, placing Indians on an equality, within the British Empire, with white citizens. She was made, by Mr. Montagu, an original member of the League of Nations,

[1] I presided in the spring of 1921 at the first Reform Conference in Malabar, and showed the work done during the first six weeks of the new Legislatures. The summary occupied 22 demi-octavo pages of print.

and wherever the Dominions were granted aught of power, he—remembering that she was not a "Dominion"—added "and India," so that, outside her own land, she has "achieved Dominion status". This is, of course, an anomaly, but an anomaly that can only end in one way. We are too near these changes and they come so rapidly, that we fail to realise the pace at which we are travelling. Those of us who have worked through long years of frustration, to some extent recognise our gains, but those who have done nothing clamour incessantly for more, knowing naught of the difficulties yet to be overcome.

It only needs a little patience and courage on the part of India to win Home Rule through the Reform Act, and Mr. Montagu, as Secretary of State, will remain glorious in Indian History, as the man who opened the gate of the road leading to Home Rule, and stood firmly by India as she began to tread it.

Nor should the Viceroy, Lord Chelmsford, be forgotten, who worked with Mr. Montagu through the initial stages, and had the courage to declare at the opening of the Indian Legislature that "autocracy was abandoned," laying down, by his own work and will, the mighty power he had wielded over more than three hundred millions of human beings. Few are the autocrats, who, like Lord Chelmsford and Mr. Montagu, being offered a great opportunity, have risen to the height of renunciation to which they attained, and, without the compulsion of Revolution, laid at the feet of a great subject Nation the splendid gift of Freedom to tread the path which led to Home Rule, working out her own salvation. The nobility of their action is not yet appreciated, for we are still struggling to reach our goal, and do but poor justice to those who have brought us within reach of it; we wanted more than they were able to obtain for us, facing the tremendous forces of race pride, consciousness of armed strength, contempt of oriental peoples, and the strong ground of possession unchallenged effectively for one hundred and sixty years, and all the wealth obtained by India's subjection. Against all these they struggled gallantly, and when India rules herself, she will do them justice and gratefully acknowledge the debt she owes them. History will write their names in golden letters, who found a Nation enslaved and set it free to win, by its own strength, its place among the Self-Governing Nations of the world. Never before has so great a Revolution been accomplished without bloodshed; never before has the autocrat voluntarily resigned power into the hands of subjects, re-created into citizens.

CHAPTER VII

THE REVOLUTIONARY MOVEMENTS

It is necessary now to leave the main current of political events, and to trace, as briefly as possible, another current which ran side by side with it, sometimes above ground, as an agitation tending to violence, sometimes below ground, as an organised and definite secret conspiracy.

In the Introduction, pp. 8, 9, I mentioned "the rise of the great Marāṭha Power," and said that the "Marāṭha Confederacy" had its centres in Poona, Nāgpūr, Indore, Gwalior and Baroda, and "practically ruled India" up to the beginning of the nineteenth century. The Marāṭhas are, in some ways, one of the most remarkable races in India, physically stalwart, virile, brave, intellectually strong and practical, emotionally proud, reserved, and even hard and imperious outside, but tender where they love, and very faithful friends. Bāl Gaṅgāḍhar Tilak was their political chief in our own days, and they never wavered in their loyalty, 'come cloud come sunshine'. He was in a very real sense their King. He was a man of brilliant brain, of indomitable will, of flawless courage, and of absolute devotion to his Motherland; a Free India was his Ideal, and he used to reach it every resource of the strategist, the diplomat, the lawyer, the soldier. "Freedom is my birthright, and I will have it" was a characteristic phrase. In India's service, his self-abnegation was perfect; but he never wavered in his aim, and he was ruthless in its pursuit. Withal, he had a sense of humour, which oftentimes stood him in good stead. To the bureaucrat such a man was intolerable; his attitude was that of Charles Bradlaugh when he fought the injustice of Parliament, and said at the Bar of the Commons' House: "You may break me, but you shall never bend me." Mr. Tilak, in the first legal attack made on him, was very unfairly treated, and when he was, in 1908, condemned for sedition and sent to six years of imprisonment, it was for language which now would be deemed fair political fighting. But those days were the days of the might of the bureaucrat, and he was too strong and too great to be left at large.

The Viceroyalty of Lord Curzon was the seed-bed of Indian Revolutionary movements. He was, as it were, a scourge in the hand of India's Ḍeva, to arouse India to a sense of her subordinate position as a mere "Dependency" of Great Britain; while he ruled her, he made her writhe under a sense of her helpless inferiority, and he gave voice to this same feeling in 1922, when he scornfully spoke of her as a subordinate branch of the Government. To such a man, naturally, B. G. Tilak, with a greater and more legitimate pride of race and a will to Freedom, was intolerable, and it was in his time that the secret drilling and arming of young volunteers was resorted to.

The Official Report of the Twenty-first National Congress, held in 1905 in Benares, summarised this unhappy Viceroyalty as follows. Never, since an earlier dark period of trouble in Indian history many years before,

> had India been so distracted, discontented, despondent; the victim of so many misfortunes, political and other; the target for so much scorn and calumny emanating from the highest quarters—its most moderate demands ridiculed and scouted, its most reasonable prayers greeted with a stiff negative, its noblest aspirations spurned and denounced as pure mischief or solemn nonsense, its most cherished ideals hurled down from their pedestal and trodden under foot—never had the condition of India been more critical than it was during the second ill-starred administration of Lord Curzon. The Official Secrets Act was passed in the teeth of universal opposition. It was condemned by the

whole Press—Indian and Anglo-Indian—protests from all quarters poured in, but Lord Curzon was implacable, and the Gagging Act was passed. Education was crippled and mutilated; it was made expensive and it was officialised; and so that most effective instrument for the enslavement of our National interest, the Indian Universities Act, was passed, and the policy of checking, if not altogether undoing, the noble work of Bentinck, Macaulay and Lord Halifax, which for more than half a century has been continued with such happy results to the country, came in full swing. *(How India Wrought for Freedom*, p. 415.*)*

Mr. Gokhale was the President of that Congress; no revolutionary he, but the calmest, most reasonable, most patient—and resolute—of Indian patriots. Here is his verdict on Lord Curzon's Viceroyalty:

Gentlemen, how true is it that to everything there is an end! Thus even the Viceroyalty of Lord Curzon has come to a close! For seven long years all eyes had constantly to turn to one masterful figure in the land—now in admiration, now in astonishment, more often in anger and in pain, till at last it has become difficult to realise that a change has really come. For a parallel to such an administration, we must, I think, go back to the times of Aurangzeb in the history of our own country. There we find the same attempt at a rule excessively centralised and intensely personal, the same strenuous purpose, the same overpowering consciousness of duty, the same marvellous capacity for work, the same sense of loneliness, the same persistence in a policy of distrust and repression, resulting in bitter exasperation all round. I think even the most devoted admirer of Lord Curzon cannot claim that he has strengthened the foundations of British rule in India. . . . To him India was a country where the Englishman was to monopolise for all time all power, and talk all the while of duty. The Indian's only business was to be governed, and it was a sacrilege on his part to have any other aspiration. In his scheme of things there was no room for the educated classes of the country; and having failed to amuse them for any length of time by an empty show of taking them into his confidence, he proceeded in the end to repress them. Even in his last farewell speech at the Byculla Club in Bombay, India exists only as a scene of the Englishman's labours, with the toiling millions of the country—eighty per cent of the population—in the background. The remaining twenty per cent, for aught they are worth, might as well be gently swept into the sea! (*Ibid.*, p. 417.)

Mentioning the remarkable men who had opposed the Partition, he said:

If the opinions of even such men are to be brushed aside with contempt, if all Indians are to be treated as no better than dumb, driven cattle; if men, whom any other country would delight to honour, are to be thus made to realise the utter humiliation and helplessness of their position in their own, then all I can say is: "Good-bye to all hope of co-operating in any way with the bureaucracy in the interests of the people!" I can conceive of no graver indictment of British rule than that such a state of things should be possible after a hundred years of that rule! (*Ibid.*, p. 418.)

Our whole future, it is needless to say, is bound up with this question of the relative position of the two races in this country. The dominance of one race over another—especially when there is no great disparity between their intellectual endowments or their general civilisation—inflicts great injury on the subject race in a thousand insidious ways. On the moral side, the present situation is steadily destroying our capacity for initiative and dwarfing us as men of action. On the material side, it has resulted in a fearful impoverishment of the people. For a hundred years and more now India has been for members of the dominant race a country where fortunes were to be made, to be taken out and spent elsewhere. As in Ireland the evil of absentee landlordism has in the past aggravated the racial domination of the English over the Irish, so in India what may be called absentee capitalism has been added to the racial ascendancy of Englishmen. A great and ruinous drain of wealth from the country has gone on for many years, the net excess of exports over imports (including treasure) during the last forty years amounting to no less than a thousand millions sterling. The steady rise in the death-rate of the country—from 24 per thousand, the average for 1882—84, to 30 per thousand, the average for 1892—94, and 34 per thousand, the present average—is a terrible and conclusive proof of this continuous impoverishment of the mass of our people. India's best interests—material and moral—no less than the honour of England, demand that the policy of equality for the two races, promised by the Sovereign and by Parliament, should be faithfully and courageously carried out. (*Ibid.*, pp. 420, 421.)

It is no wonder that, with such a record, Lord Curzon should have been a bitter enemy of Mr. Montagu and his Reforms, for a man who despised Indians as an inferior race could not but fight against one who recognised them, as of right, as equal partners in the Empire.

The first of the Revolutionary Movements of our time grew out of the treatment of Mr. Tilak in Mahārāshṭra, and out of the Partition of Bengal. In the latter Presidency, the youths of the better classes were the chief agents, and they were most skilfully organised, on the old German model, into groups, the members of which did not know each other, but only knew their chief. They met at night for a dacoity, and scattered when it was over. Lots were cast for the agent for an assassination, the order was given, and executed. And while this was going on, Germany—intent on world domination, and with her agents in every country working for the destruction of the British Empire, the great obstacle in her way—saw her opportunity, and supplied money and arms; a rising in India was planned for "the Day," and skilfully prepared for. Her other agency was the German missionary and his schools; in vain I warned the public of the growing danger, where children talked of "our Kaiser" and "your Emperor," and were thus prepared to become revolutionaries in the colleges. A curious side attack came against me personally, which turned out to be part of the Pan-German world-conspiracy, to deprive me of the Presidentship of the world-wide Theosophical Society and to instal a German in my stead. It is only now, since the far-flung German preparations to destroy the British Empire have become known, that we can see the links so skilfully woven. In the spring of 1911, India was flooded by a "storm of obloquy and vituperation" directed against Theosophy, and against myself as President of the Theosophical Society, on which I remarked that "one marvels to see [as a result] some retardation only and no wreckage" (Presidential Address, 1911, p. 4). In Germany itself was a powerful movement under Dr. Rudolf Steiner, to silence all Theosophical teaching except his own German form thereof. An emissary from the American assailants came to me in India, representing himself as coming from the head of the

Theosophical organisation that had been attacking me, and expressing regret. I did not then know that this gentleman, Mr. Myrom Phelps, was "a well-known supporter of the anarchistic movement connected with India House in New York, whence *Free Hinḍusthān* was issued," and that he was travelling in India, making friends chiefly with the Extremist party, who probably did not know his American work. He came to Madras, and the above-named furious attack on Theosophy, and then on me, followed, in which a close friend of his was the leader. In Germany the attack increased in violence, and in the later part of the year books were published in France, Great Britain and America against me, trying to drive me into resignation, and suggesting Dr. Rudolf Steiner as my successor. Needless to say how well it would have served Germany to have had a Pan-German at the centre of a world-wide Society, with members in nearly all civilised countries. I weathered the storm, and a breach of the T. S. Constitution in Germany enabled me to cancel its Charter, and to revive it for those who were willing to work within the T. S. (Presidential Address, 1912, pp. 3—17, and 1913, pp. 3—7).

Only later, when the War broke out, when the Ghaḍr conspiracy in California—whence the worst attacks had issued—was unmasked, and the flight of some connected with it to Berlin proved the nature of the work carried on by Germans here, did I realise the connection between them and the troubles in the Theosophical Society in 1911, '12, and '13, culminating in the attempt to seat a German at Adyar in its Headquarters. But the links between the T.S. and the place of India in a World-Empire, or Federation, of Free Nations, have existed since the Society came here, and under the guidance of her Ṛṣhis, India has been winning her way to Ordered Liberty, and has not yet diverged wholly into the Path of Revolution. But her Destiny is now in the balance.

The Defence of India Act, 1915, was aimed chiefly, as said in its objects, at the definite revolutionary movements in the Panjāb and in Bengal. The Panjāb movement was largely Sīkh, resulting from trouble in connection with the going to Canada of an emigrant ship, the Komagatu, and its return to Calcutta, a riot resulting among its passengers after landing. The movement was crushed in the Panjāb, but the harsh and oppressive rule of Sir Michael O'Dwyer, his press-gang methods of recruitment, his forced War Loans, and his cruel persecution of all political leaders, kept the covered-up embers of resentment alive, and ready to break into flame. At the Special Congress of 1918, in Bombay, Panjābi delegates told us how they were living over a volcano, which any act of exceptional tyranny might cause to burst out. We were not therefore surprised when open trouble occurred in 1919 in this very Province.

I will ask the reader to refer to the description of the state of high tension in which India was living since 1914: her enthusiasm at the beginning of the War; the hopes excited by the voiced gratitude of Britain for her eager help in the first days in September, 1914; the strenuous exhortations and uplifted ideals by western statesmen; then the increasing War-pressure, leading to huge loans and strong endeavours to recruit men, especially in the North, which, as said, became exasperated by the ill-government of Sir Michael O'Dwyer; the unwise use of the Press Act and Defence of India Act to put down the advocates of political Reform; the huge number of mostly young internees and the cruelly harsh treatment meted out to them, with the insecurity of liberty and property to which every Reformer was exposed and the consequent distrust and suspicion which spread over the educated classes as witness Sir James Meston in 1919; the hopes raised by the Declaration of August 20, 1917, and the disappointment over the Reform proposals; the rejection of a Home Rule deputation, sent to counter the dangerous agitation against India in England. To all this must be added the effect of the world-unrest, of the fallen thrones of Europe, of the insurrectionary movements there, of the up-springing of new Nations and the justifying of the freedom of Nationalities, white in colour but by no means so civilised as India; all this caused an unexampled state of feeling in India—and into this was thrown, early in 1919, the Rowlatt Bill.

The provisions of this, as first drafted, raised a storm of protests: Was this England's answer at the end of the War (the Armistice had been signed in November, 1918) to the

India that had fought for her in every theatre of battle since 1914, this proof of distrust in her loyalty, nay, of the insincerity of her talk about Reforms and Liberty? A number of us resolved that we would ignore the Bill when it became law, disregarding its impossible restrictions: I wrote against it in *New India*, spoke against it on the platform, as did all other leaders in the Reform struggle; we had asked for Reform, and we were given harsher repression. The fight against it in the Viceroy's Legislative Council modified largely the objectionable measure, though not depriving it of its fundamental fault—the substitution of Executive for Judicial action. But it left nothing we could disregard as a protest, unless we were revolutionaries, and then, as said above, Mr. Gandhi determined on entering on a campaign of passive resistance by breaking other laws (see p. 201). To break other non-tyrannous laws, which one had hitherto obeyed, because a new tyrannous law had in it no clause that one could righteously disregard, seemed to me illogical and absurd. Besides such a policy was certain to give rise, among the ignorant and the criminal, to general lawlessness, destructive of all government and fatal to Society. I wrote a series of articles on the sanctity of Law, and I broke, as said above, with Mr. Gandhi and his party. He devised and proclaimed a "hartal"—a total cessation of business of every kind—for April 6. In some places it was carried out peaceably, in others with violence, and a dangerous riot broke out in Delhi, resulting in bloodshed—the first bloodshed in this disastrous campaign. It was the signal for the outburst we had feared in the Panjāb, and some very bad rioting took place also in the northern part of the Bombay Presidency, but there it was skilfully defeated, no undue severity was used, and no feeling of revenge was left. In Amritsar, on April 11, two popular leaders were arrested and carried away; a crowd, unarmed and peaceful, with the usual Hinḍū signs of mourning, went towards the Civil Lines to ask whither they had gone; they were stopped by soldiers, and sat down on the ground, mourning. In a foolish panic, they were fired on, and several were slain. It was the signal for an outburst of mad rage. The crowd picked up sticks and bars, rushed back into the town and attacked banks, Government buildings, the railway station; some five Englishmen were killed, an Englishwoman was assailed and beaten, but rescued by some Indians. By the evening, all was quiet again. On the next day, many arrests were made, and there was no resistance; all was peace; the sudden rage provoked by the foolish firing had died down, and there need have been no more trouble. But troops had been sent for, and General Dyer and his men arrived on the evening of the 12th. On the next day, Sunday, April 13, he went through a few streets, and forbade any meetings. A meeting had been arranged for that day in a large open space, Jallianwala Bagh, and people came, a holiday crowd, from all the surrounding country. General Dyer was told a crowd was gathering, and he did nothing. Jallianwala Bagh was a walled-in space, with some five narrow outlets. When 20,000 people had gathered in it, he marched down with machine-guns, but even the widest of the passages was too narrow for their entry. He had 40 men, with a supply of ammunition, and the ground sloped down slightly from his station. He gave the order to fire into the crowd, and himself directed the fire so as to close the small outlets with dead and dying, as the amazed and panic-stricken crowd fled before the hail of bullets, men, women, little children —tiny shoes of children in arms were found scattered about afterwards. When his ammunition was exhausted, he and his soldiers marched away, leaving the ground strewn with dead and wounded. As he said afterwards, that was not his "job"; he meant to give a lesson. None might be out after dark, on pain of death; there were no doctors; the wounded lay through the terrible heat of the night, a few brave persons creeping in with water—a mere drop in the ocean of thirst. Then came worse.

The educated people over the district were rounded up, thrown into prison, handcuffed in pairs, night and day fastened together without break for washing or necessary demands of nature: in the lane where the Englishwoman was beaten, men and young boys were flogged to insensibility, taken down, flogged again, to obtain evidence of the attack on her, of which they knew nothing; all Indians who had to pass through that lane, residents and all, had to wriggle along through it on their stomachs, and were struck or prodded with bayonets if they tried to raise themselves a little ; the cruelties, the shocking humiliations, the tortures, the farcical trials with preposterous sentences, the bombs dropped on any groups of people, members of a wedding party flogged as an unlawful gathering, villages raided, property burnt, men shot or flogged, women insulted—it was a hell of wickedness. An iron ring was kept round the shambles, within which every educated man was baited and illused, and the outside world knew naught; Sir Michael O'Dwyer at last had his way.

When the facts leaked out, India went mad with pity, grief and horror. And yet, for all the boiling wrath, Indians were just. They did not take revenge, but they asked for justice, and that justice was denied. Out of the passions roused by that new wrong grew the movement of Non-Co-Operation, started definitely on April 9, 1920. The passive resistance movement of 1919 was stopped by Mr. Gandhi after the Delhi rioting and the outbreak in the north of the Bombay Presidency, as he held it to be "a Himālayan blunder" to have expected self-control from the masses of the people, and he recognised that lawlessness had been caused by it in 1919.

But the lesson was forgotten, and he started again the Non-Co-Operation movement, against which we raised and maintained a steady campaign. The story is outlined in the following Foreword of a booklet, containing articles and speeches of the leaders in the struggle for Reform against Revolution. I wrote:

> This booklet is a collection of articles, written by a number of well-known persons, against the fatal policy of Non-Co-Operation, which is daily becoming more and more violent; if it be not checked by the resolute opposition of the thoughtful, it will crush the country by necessitating repression, or drive it into a welter of anarchy, a National suicide.
>
> Mr. Gandhi, the leader of this crusade, has gone through a number of changes with bewildering

rapidity. At the end of December, 1919, he proposed, but did not ultimately move, in the National Congress, a resolution promising Co-operation in reply to the King-Emperor's message, and finally agreed to a compromise resolution, not promising Co-operation, but directing the working of the Reforms with a view to obtain Self-Government.

In January, February and the first half of March, the attention of the country was focussed on the Reforms, and the political lectures delivered were directed towards educating the electorates for their new and responsible duties. Personally I worked hard at this, carrying on a regular campaign to popularise the Reforms. But side by side with this, a movement grew up among the Musalmāns, who became much disturbed over the Khilāfat and Turkey, and Mr. Gandhi made common cause with them, and with them formulated his ultimately famous four progressive steps of Non-Co-Operation.

A Khilāfat Committee was formed early in 1920, and meetings were called to express sympathy with Turkey. On March 9 one was held in Madras, with the Hon. Mr. Yakub Hasan in the Chair, and Mr. Kastūriraṅga Iyengar, Mr. S. Saṭyamūrti and many Hinḍū gentlemen were present. Mr. Montagu was praised by the Chairman, who said that he had suggested to him a powerful federation of Muslim States, which the British Government would help and with which it would co-operate. Resolutions were passed pledging unswerving loyalty and devotion to the Khalifa and stating that

> no terms that do not vouchsafe to the Turks the full and independent sovereignty over their Homeland in Europe and Asia, and to the Sultān the suzerainty over Arabia, Palestine, Syria and Mesopotamia, thus maintaining his position as Khalifa, the custodian and guardian of the Holy Places of Islām, can ever be acceptable to India that has helped the Allies to win the War.

A hartal was proposed for March 19, and Mr. Gandhi issued a manifesto strongly urging that there should be no violence and that it should be absolutely voluntary. He suggested that if the Turkish Treaty should be unsatisfactory, "there should be no violence in thought, speech, or deed, no boycott of British goods, as it is one form of violence, and no mixing of other questions with the Khilāfat, such as the Egyptian question"; people holding offices of honour and emolument under Government and menial Government servants should resign. "Non-Co-Operation with the Government, free from all things of violence, is the only effective remedy open to the people." "No threat of ostracism should be used and the withdrawal of Co-operation should be purely voluntary." He spoke very strongly against violence:

> I should cease to co-operate and advise every Hinḍū and for that matter everyone else to cease to co-operate, the moment there was violence actually done, advised or countenanced. I would therefore urge upon all speakers the exercise of the greatest restraint under the gravest provocation. There is certainty of victory, if firmness is combined with gentleness. The cause is doomed if anger, hatred, ill-will, recklessness, and finally

violence are to reign supreme. I shall resist them with my life, even if I should stand alone. My goal is friendship with the world, and I can combine the greatest love with the greatest opposition to wrong. (*New India*, March 10, 1920. See also March 11.)

Such was Mr. Gandhi in March, 1920.

Events thenceforth moved rapidly, Khilāfat Committees were formed and meetings held. The Khilāfat Offices in Calcutta were raided on March 14. The deputation which had gone to England with the Viceroy's help, kept in touch with India, and the crusade against the Turks in England during March embittered Musalmān feeling in India; the Madras Provincial Congress Committee called on all to take part in the hartal of March 19, and some prominent Hindūs and Musalmāns in Madras issued a joint appeal (*New India*, March 17). There was a great and peaceful response all over India on March 19, and only in Burma was any repression used. *New India*, in a leading article on March 20, pointed out that underlying the Khilāfat question was the question of European aggression on Asia, and that all Indians were one in objecting to Asian civilisation being engulfed by European, and in claiming equality for Asiatic and European.

A National Week, commemorating the Panjāb atrocities was opened on April 6 by meetings at which all parties were represented. The main request made on April 6 was that the Rowlatt Act should be repealed; Mr. Gandhi declared at Bombay that if the Rowlatt Act were not repealed before the inauguration of the Reforms the demand made on them for Co-operation would be futile, and he, for one, would find the situation such as to make remaining within the Empire impossible (*New India*, April 7). The Khilāfat does not appear to have been noticed in the resolutions passed; collections for the Jallianwala Bagh Memorial were pressed. But April 9, within the week, was fixed as "Khilāfat Day," and on this a resolution was passed in Bombay and elsewhere, moved in Bombay by Mr. Gandhi, declaring that if the just demands of Musalmāns were not agreed to,

> and in the event of any adverse decision being arrived at, it will be the duty of every Indian to withdraw Co-operation from Government until pledges are fulfilled and Muslim sentiment conciliated.

Thus was the fatal note struck, and the real Non-Co-Operation campaign was begun on April 9, 1920.

In *The Citizen* of Madras and in *New India*, simultaneously, appeared, on April 10, Sir P. S. Sivaswami Iyer's article, "The Khilāfat Situation," the first answer to the challenge; it is printed here on p. 3, as the opening article of our collection. On April 15, 16, 20 and 21 it was followed by Mrs. Annie Besant's four articles on "Co-operation or Non-Co-Operation," and "Conscience," "The Present Crisis" and "A True Saṭyāgrahi," unfortunately overlooked when the collection was made; they are printed as an Appendix. The great Khilāfat

Demonstration in Madras was held on April 17, and Mr. Gandhi's famous four progressive steps in Non-Co-Operation were passed as a resolution:

> In consonance with the spirit of the Resolution adopted by the All-India Khilāfat Committee, this Conference, in the event of the present agitation proving futile and ineffective, calls upon all Indians to resort to progressive abstention from Co-operation with Government in the following manner:
>
> Firstly, to renounce all honorary posts, titles and memberships of Legislative Councils.
>
> Secondly, to give up all remuneratory posts under Government service.
>
> Thirdly, to give up all appointments in the Police and Military forces.
>
> Fourthly to refuse to pay taxes to Government.

This was proposed by Moulvi Abdul Majid Sharar, seconded by Mr. S. Kastūriraṅga Iyengar, supported by Messrs. S. Satyamūrti, C. Rājagopālāchāriār, A. Raṅgaswāmi Iyengar, M. K. Āchāriār, Paṇḍiṭ Bansi Dhar and several Musalmāns. The President of the Conference, Moulana Shaukat Ali, added after reciting the four steps: "We do not embark on this step without fully realising what it means. It means a movement for absolute independence." At that time, Mr. Gandhi did not go so far, but some of us clearly saw that the movement was definitely revolutionary, despite its sheep's clothing. From this time onwards *New India* kept up a fairly constant fusillade, and I wrote other articles in *The Citizen*, *The Servant of India*, *The Leader* and *The Looker-on*.

The Hon. Mr. V. S. Srinivâsa Sâstri joined in the fray on May 15 in *The Citizen,* and Mr. Jamnaḍâs Ḍwârkaḍâs—now a member of the Indian Legislative Assembly—in *The Bombay Chronicle.*

After the Congress the Hon. Mr. R. P. Paranjpe, Mr. C. P. Râmaswâmi Aiyar and I myself wrote in *The Servant of India;* Mr. Ambika Charan Mozumdar and later Sir A. Chaudhuri and Messrs. Satyananda Bose, J. N. Roy, J. Chaudhuri and B. C. Chatterji addressed the readers of *The Bengalee;* Mr. G. A. Natesan those of *The Indian Review*; the Hon. Mr. Bhurgi those of *The New Times*; and Mr. N. M. Samarth those of *The Asiatic Review.*

The meeting of the All-India Congress Committee at Benares, on May 30 and 31, marked a new departure. It will be remembered that Mr. Gandhi, in March had forbidden the mixing up of Non-Co-Operation in defence of the Khilâfat with other questions; but it was found that the Khilâfat was not sufficiently attractive to Hinḍûs, so at Benares the Panjâb Atrocities and the deficiencies of the Reform Act were added to the provocative causes. On June 1 at Allahabad, another grave addition was made—the creation of a Council, the directions of which were to be obeyed in action and abstention from action, practically a Council of War. An ultimatum was sent to the Viceroy, giving him a month's grace, and August 1 was proclaimed as the day on which Non-Co-Operation was definitely to begin with Step No. 1. The response was poor, but fiery discussion went on all over the country.

On September 4, the Special Congress began, and after long discussion a resolution was formulated approving Mr. Gandhi's progressive policy, and amplifying Step No. 1 in detail. Over 3,000 delegates abstained from voting, 1,826 voted with Mr. Gandhi, 884 for Mr. Pāl's amendment, and 63 objected to both or were neutral. The resolution was sent to a Sub-Committee of the All-India Congress Committee, amended by that body and published. Most of the Bengal, Madras and Bombay leaders, who had voted against Mr. Gandhi, submitted to the so-called "mandate" of the Congress on the Boycott of Council clause alone. A handful of lawyers have given up their practice; no one appears to boycott foreign goods. Mr. Gandhi himself uses railways, post, telegraph and motor cars. The failure of the propaganda has led to extraordinary violence of language, now passing into the breaking up of meetings. Mr. Gandhi and the two "Ali Brothers" in despair, have attacked Aligarh and Benares Universities and the Sikh Khalsa College. Aligarh has, after a struggle, held its own; no serious attack has been made on the other two, but Khalsa College has withdrawn from Government control.

The Liberals and National Home Rulers joined forces in educating the voters on the Reform Act, and have been actively co-operating against the dangerous Non-Co-Operation Crusade.

This booklet is issued to give weapons to the combatants. The battle is joined, and as when the old knightly warriors charged, and met in shock of conflict, we cry with the Herald:

"GOD DEFEND THE RIGHT!"

November 17, 1920 ANNIE BESANT

The fourfold programme was begun formally on August 1, 1920; Swarāj was to be attained in a year, and on August 1, 1921, the first step was taken in the Malabar Rebellion; the Musalmāns (Moplas) of that district after three weeks of preparing weapons, rose over a definite area in revolt, believing, as they had been told, that British Rule had ceased, and they were free; they established the Khilāfat Rāj, crowned a King, murdered and plundered abundantly, and killed or drove away all Hindūs who would not apostatise. Somewhere about a lakh (100,000) of people were driven from their homes with nothing but the clothes they had on, stripped of everything. Some thousands of Moplas have been killed fighting. Many thousands more have been wounded and are prisoners. The misery caused has been indescribable, the crimes, the tortures, unspeakable. The Khilāfat preachers have the greatest share of the guilt; the Congressmen, with their violence abuse of the Government, their lawlessness, their declarations that they were out to "destroy the Government," were "at war with the Government," a large share. An ignorant, fanatical, Musalmān people interpreted destruction and war in the only sense of the words they knew, and carried them out against "the enemies of Islām". In March, 1922, the refugees are slowly returning to their ruined homes and devastated fields, but some parts are still unsafe.

The changes of programme have been kaleidoscopic; as soon as one failed, another was invented; Swarāj was to arrive on September 30 or October 1, 1921; on October 31; on December 31 at the Congress; it is as far off as ever. A feeble attempt was made to persuade Musalmāns to leave the army and the police, and then Mr. Gandhi proclaimed it to be sinful for any Indian to be in either force. Nothing happened, except that in connection with their propaganda of incitement to violence and tampering with the troops Moulanas Muhammad Ali and Shaukat Ali are in prison. Mr. Gandhi always preached non-violence, but wherever his followers stirred up the people violence ensued, and a habit of violence has been set up. Sir Sankaran Nair gives a list of 92 riots, 87 of which some very serious, which occurred between January, 1921 and February, 1922. These were not all directly connected with Non-Co-Operation, but were signs of the spreading inclination to resort to violence on slight provocation, and of the growing disregard of all authority. The enrolment of volunteers and picketing have been fruitful in minor assaults, and the volunteers have proved veritable tyrants, stopping trade, breaking up meetings, and behaving in the rowdy mischievous ways common to schoolboys who have thrown off all discipline.

Under the Gandhi Rāj there is no Free Speech, no open Meeting, unless for Non-Co-Operators. Social and Religious boycott, threats of personal violence, spitting, insults in the streets, are the methods of suppression. Mob support is obtained by wild promises, such as the immediate coming of Swarāj, when there will be no rents, no taxes, by giving to Mr. Gandhi high religious names, such as Mahāṭmā and Avaṭāra, assigning to him supernatural powers, and the like. Abraham Lincoln is alleged to have said that you could fool all the people for some time. Mr. Gandhi has certainly succeeded in fooling a part of them. He asks for two million spinning-wheels for 2 million families, and later he wants 48 millions. The spinning wheel is the Saviour of India. In consequence of unkind suggestions that men could not be clothed by thread alone, he added handlooms, and just now hand-woven cloth is the salvation of India. Foreign cloth is boycotted or burnt. If there is not cloth enough to go round—and there is not—what there is must be cut up, and each man must have only a loin-cloth; Mr. Gandhi promptly sheds his clothes, and goes about in a loin-cloth only. Husbands and wives must live apart, to prevent slave children being born into the world. Hospitals are "institutions for propagating sin". Doctors try to cure diseases caused by evil-living and so encourage it. Railways, machinery, are all bad. Man is restricted by nature to move as far as his hands and feet will take him, and he rushes about on railways. And so on, *ad infinitum.* This is Mr. Gandhi's Gospel, as witness his book on *Indian Home Rule.* And all this midsummer madness has caught the fancy of boys and illiterates, and they shout down the rationals. When, at last, Mr. Gandhi took the serious step of calling out millions of volunteers, and bade people pay no taxes, the Government arrested him, tried him in the politest way and sent him to gaol. He now advises people to take up a programme of social work, which raises no enthusiasm after all the excitement, says that all his followers who have gone to prison (for violence of talk or of act) "must be sacrificed," so that presumably they will serve out their sentences, and he is devoting himself to learning Urdu. He says that he finds that he cannot control the forces he has raised, and is, presumably, rather glad to be relieved from the necessity of trying to do so.

Most of the large number of Non-Co-Operators who are in gaol are there for refusing to give security to abstain from violent language or meetings in forbidden areas. They take up the position that they do not recognise the courts and will not plead. Some of the leaders are there for sedition. Curiously, except for a few newspapers, who rave against the Government, no one seems to be particularly troubled about any of them. The Revolution, for the moment is stationary, but Revolutions cannot stand still and live. So far as Mr. Gandhi's real followers are concerned —they are a small, well-organised minority, they are honestly non-violent, and perfectly harmless, so far as Government is concerned, except that their very inflammatory speech, exciting others. They are told no longer to break laws, no longer to "court going to gaol," to produce, sell and buy Khaddar (handwoven cloth). They do so. The Government is justified by this statement implying that they did break laws, and courted imprisonment, and leaves them there. The crowd looks on, and finding no amusement, does nothing, there being no one to lead it into mischief.

It is the queerest Revolution that ever was, since Gandhi replaced Tilak, has had the queerest leader, and has now the queerest collapse.

And meanwhile the Legislatures are justifying themselves by work. By the time Mr. Gandhi comes out, all his rational followers will have returned to Politics, and it is even quite likely that we may have reached Home Rule.

CHAPTER VIII

SELF-DETERMINATION AND SELF-GOVERNMENT

IN all countries which are unfree, a stage is reached in which the unfree Nation becomes Self-conscious, and demands the right to make her own path "according to the Word," that is according to the fragment of Divinity which is her Self, the Inner Ruler Immortal, the Deity of whom she is one of the National embodiments. As truly as the Self in an individual is the unspringing source of Life within him, that gradually brings his embodiment into subjection to his will, to be the instrument of his activities, shaping and moulding it into Self-expression, so is there a National Self, a National Life, shaping and moulding the external mind, emotions and physical body of the Nation into Self-expression, that she may speak her own letter of the Name, sound her own note in the Chord, which is the Self-expression of the Lord of her world. The individuality of the Nation is as much a truth as the individuality of the man.

Usually an unfree Nation is young, ruled over by one of its own race, or conquered and held by another; in the first case as it reaches Self-consciousness it grows into Freedom; in the second, it throws off the yoke by a successful rebellion. India is unique, in that she is a very ancient Nation, not Self-conscious as a whole in the land she dwelt in, save in her religion and her intellect, in the region of her spiritual and cultural life; moreover she was gradually rendered unfree in a period of lassitude and division by the co-operation of some of her peoples with a young and energetic Nation. Hence, in her present Self-consciousness, she is not a minor, under tutelage of a guardian older and wiser than herself, but a mature Nation, re-awakened from a temporary loss of consciousness, finding herself somewhat unnaturally discomforted by foreign and in many ways unsuitable garments, put on her during her trance. To be treated as a child irritates her, and makes her restless and uneasy. But she finds it difficult to express herself in an authoritative fashion, having lost her old organs of speech, and not having sufficiently proved her new ones. Hence in the National Congress at Delhi, in December, 1920, in view of the coming changes, the following resolution was proposed by myself, seconded by Mr. C. R. Das, and supported by Mr. Barkat Ali, Mr. Jamnaḍās Ḍwārkaḍās, Dr. Kitchlew, Mr. Saṭyamūrṭi, Paṇḍiṭ Gokarannāṭh, and Dr. Chasṭhi Ram.

Mrs. Sarojini Naidu was one of the chosen speakers, but was absent unwell. It was carried unanimously and ran as follows:

XI. In view of the pronouncement of President Wilson, Mr. Lloyd George, and other British statesmen, that to ensure the future peace of the world, the principle of Self-Determination should be applied to all progressive Nations,

Be it resolved—

1. That this Congress claims the recognition of India by the British Parliament and by the Peace Conference as one of the progressive Nations, to whom the principle of Self-Determination should be applied.

2. That in practical application of the principle in India the first step should be—

(*a*) The removal of all hindrances to free discussion, and therefore the immediate repeal of all laws, regulations and ordinances restricting the free discussion of political questions, whether in the press, private or public meeting, or otherwise, so that the legitimate aspirations and opinions of all residents in India may be fearlessly expressed; further, the abolition of the laws, regulations and ordinances, which confer on the Executive the power to arrest, detain, intern, extern, or imprison any British subject in India, outside the processes of ordinary Civil or Criminal Law, and the assimilation of the law of sedition to that of England.

(*b*) The passing of an Act of Parliament which will establish at an early date complete Responsible Government in India.

(*c*) When complete Responsible Government shall be thus established, the final authority in all internal affairs shall be the supreme Legislative Assembly as voicing the will of the Indian Nation.

Resolved further—

(*d*) That in the reconstruction of Imperial policy, whether in matters affecting the inner relations of the Nations constituting it, in questions of foreign policy, or in the League of Nations, India shall be accorded the same position as the Self-Governing Dominions.

The statement made by President Wilson, alluded to in the preamble, was:

One of the four ends for which the associated people of the world are fighting is the settlement of every question, whether of territory, sovereignty, of economic arrangement, or of political relationship upon the basis of the free acceptance of that settlement by the people immediately concerned, and not upon the basis of the material interest or advantage of any other nation or people which may desire a different settlement for the sake of its own exterior influence or mastery.

The statement of Mr. Lloyd George was:

> The leading principle is that the wishes of the inhabitants must be the supreme consideration in the resettlement. In other words, the formula adopted by the Allies in regard to the disputed territories in Europe is to be applied equally in tropical countries.

It is obvious that while the statement of President Wilson cannot bind the Government of Great Britain, that of Mr. Lloyd George, who is still Premier of Great Britain, does bind it, and the resettlement, giving Responsible Government according to the wishes of the inhabitants of India, is not yet made.

As regards the preliminaries to the practical application of the principle to India, (*a*) is almost completed. As we have seen, nearly all the hindrances to free discussion have been repealed, and the one and a half law that remains was only retained because of the unexampled licence of speech used by the leading Non-Co-Operators with the avowed intent of paralysing or destroying the Government, so as to force it to yield to a noisy but unrepresentative minority. The power of the Executive to arrest, etc., outside the ordinary "Civil or Criminal Law" has been taken away completely. The assimilation of the Indian to the English law of sedition has not yet been carried out.

(*b*) This we are asking for, and are trying to hasten it by using every power within the present Reform Act. I may add that I think the Act establishing complete Responsible Government in India should not lay down its form, but should leave India free to shape that form according to her own traditions and her own National genius. She does not want to be presented with a ready-made suit of foreign material, but would prefer to be her own tailor. (*c*) of course depends on (*b*). (*d*) may be said to be accomplished; India has a voice equal to that of the Dominions in the Imperial Conference, and questions of foreign policy are not yet submitted to the Dominions; she is, like them, an original member of the League of Nations. As Mr. Montagu said: "India has Dominion status abroad." It is still to be gained at Home.

The question of the form of Self-Government, of Home Rule, desired by India can only be determined by India herself and the matter ought to be thoroughly discussed. Much can be done under the present Act by the Governor-General, or the Provincial Governor, as the case may be, co-operating with the elected members of their respective Legislatures. Complete Provincial Autonomy could be brought about in a few months by an amendment of the Reform Act (Government of India Act, 1919) or by an amendment of the Rule which makes Councillors irresponsible. But as Parliament is not inclined to amend its Act so soon, and as British public opinion is much irritated just now by the insulting behaviour of Non-Co-Operators to the Prince of Wales, applications to England may be better left aside. A preferable method is to persuade Governors to treat all subjects as though they were transferred, as Mr. Montagu suggested during the sitting of the Joint Committee in 1919, and to invite Councillors to behave as though they were responsible. The latter invitation would probably not be accepted at first. One most important innovation has just been made by the Governor of Madras, as he has transferred from an English Councillor to an Indian one the portfolios dealing with Law and Order, Law and Justice (Criminal and Civil), the Police, including the C. I. D., State Prisoners, and Reports on matters of political importance. It is the administration of these portfolios by foreign hands which has given rise to more resentment, bad feeling and distrust than any other department of the Government, and the entrusting of them to an Indian will be welcomed with great satisfaction. Besides, it breaks down what has hitherto always been held to be the prerogative of the Englishman in India.

The number and assignment of portfolios in the Indian Government should also be reconsidered. There is no solid reason why an Education portfolio should continue, since Education is a transferred subject in the Provinces, and the little that is kept in the hands of a member of the Governor-General's Executive Council might well follow the rest to the Provinces. The portfolios of Commerce, Industry, Transport, Home, and either Law or Finance, preferable the latter, should be assigned to the Indian Members of the Council. The votes of the Assembly on the Civil Budget should be accepted as binding by the Governor-General. He has, as a matter of fact, accepted them, despite the very large reductions made in the two Budgets laid before the Reformed Councils, so that a good beginning of a convention of the complete power of the purse in civil matters has been made. The Assembly has changed the tariff to the great advantage of India and the great wrath of Lancashire, and its exercise of fiscal autonomy has been supported by the Governor-General and the Secretary of State. Although it has been held in England by the Law Officers of the Crown that the Governor-General has no power to submit the Military Budget to the vote of the Assembly, and their decision is binding for the present, leading Indian lawyers do not agree with them. The leader of the National Party in the Assembly, however, made suggestions of retrenchments in the Military Budget to the amount of nearly six crores, and the Finance Member has promised to bring them before the Retrenchment Committee, and that is a good way of obtaining control by a side-wind. The immense proportion of the revenue of India spent on the Army is an ever-increasing burden and an ever-increasing scandal. It is absolutely necessary to decrease the number of English soldiers, whose cost is out of all proportion to their value. A country should be defended by its own men and not by foreigners. And it is this which is the one real difficulty in the way of Home Rule. I have always urged that complete Home Rule should include Home Defence, and the dignity, the self-respect and the safety of India depend on the Indianisation of her army. This is one of the questions which cannot wait. It is argued by soldiers that officers cannot be trained in less than forty years, but in the

War privates who showed inborn military genius were given commissions and rose rapidly in rank. It is true that peace conditions differ from those of war, but patriotic enthusiasm for Home Rule will exert a stimulus which will go far to quicken military training. The Dehra Dun Military College is now available for embryo officers; the University Corps are intended to train young men for officers' commissions in the Territorial Armies. Officers from Indian States might be indented on, as Indian Civilians are now indented on for civil officers in those States, where they have had an opportunity hitherto denied to them in the British Rāj of showing high capacity for administration. It is true that an officer more quickly trained may not be educated up to all the minutiæ of his ceremonial duties. But the conquering armies of Napoleon showed how rapidly officers who could command on the fie d of battle could be evolved under the stress of the necessity for defending their country, and India will need her armies for self-defence, and not for aggressive warfare. The perils she will have to meet are those of raiding tribes, or at the worst of Afghāns ; China will have enough to do within her own borders for very many years to come, and under the new compact made at Washington, Japan will scarcely have a navy sufficient to transport and maintain communications with an invading army so far from her own base. Russia is no longer a danger ; and the new Arab States are too unsettled and too divided to maintain a well-concerted war. Islām is a possible danger, but that is better guarded against by the education of Musalmāns in India than by preparing to fight Musalmāns abroad, for the danger here is from ignorance and consequent fanaticism, inflamed by the insidious use of isolated passages from *Al Qurān*, given in other times and under other circumstances. They will cease to be incitements to violence, murder and forcible conversion when they can no longer be revived and utilised for political purposes, as they have been long ignored while "unbelievers" have settled for generations in the "Island of Arabia," and as similar passages in the Hebrew Scriptures, accepted by Christians, are ignored for all practical purposes, and a Christian who used them practically would be looked on as a dangerous madman. But this must depend on education, and it is the backwardness of the Musalmān masses in education which makes them so volcanic a peril to-day, uncontrollable by their own educated minority, and at the mercy of a number of fanatical Ulemas, ignorant of the present world-conditions and issuing Middle-Age fatwas, utilised by clever and ambitious Muslims, whose religion is a cloak for their political objects.

Leaving to the next chapter the question whether India shall become a country living in isolated independence, or a Free Nation in a Commonwealth of Free Nations, federated together for mutual help and protection, we may here consider whether it is preferable that India should shape her own form of Home Rule, or accept a constitution shaped by Great Britain.

I elect for the first of these alternatives, partly because Democracy, as it is shaping itself in the West, does not tend to make the people either prosperous or happy. Power has passed into the hands of multi-headed ignorance, which, with no knowledge of far-reaching international questions, selects the men who are entrusted with their solution. How the Wise are to be placed in the seats of Power, so that each Nation may be served by its best men, best in unselfish service, in high ideals, in intellect, in experience and in character, that is the question of the Sphinx, posed to modern Democracy, on the solution of which its existence depends. The white races, so far, have succeeded but poorly in their democratic ventures, and are rather examples of "how not to do it," than of admirable social and political organisation. Is there one country in Europe to-day, which is a pattern that India can safely imitate? Britain is in perpetual unrest, with continual strikes paralysing her industries and adding to the crushing weight of her unemployed, who consume but do not produce, a heavier burden than the comparatively few of the "idle rich" of former days, and by their number a greater menace to the stability of the State. Ireland, given freedom, continues to be a scene of murder and outrage, and is drifting into civil war. Is Britain, in such a condition, fit to construct a constitution for a country she does not understand? I elect for that first alternative also, because Britain and India have behind them a past of different religions, different traditions, different ideals, different customs, different social arrangements, and while they may immensely help each other by blending what is good in each, such a blending does not consist in imposing on one a type of political constitution which has grown up in the other. Saxon England and India might have evolved together, but the feudalism, the militarism and the industrialism through which Britain has reached her present political condition have no parallels in India. Britain's present has grown out of her past; India's present must likewise rest on the foundations of her past.

Lastly, I elect for that first alternative, because a stable constitution must be laid on the foundation of social obligation, on duty, and India's supreme ideal of Society has been Ḍharma, based on the relationship of all lives as rooted in the One Life, interdependent, so that Society is a complex of mutual obligations, with the family as the unit. The West, on the contrary, started from an imaginary and impossible idea of man as a solitary; an individual clothed with certain rights, and Society as an arrangement of mutual convenience whereby the rights of each are balanced with the rights of the rest, and Society with an individual as the unit is a legal creation rather than a natural growth. The theory and its working out tend to conflicts rather than to peace, to unstable rather than to stable equilibrium. Either theory, exaggerated to excess works mischief, the first producing a fossil, the second a rebel.

If the second alternative be chosen, then we should proceed to work the present Reforms to the utmost, gaining power by establishing conventions, as we are already doing, and pressing for amendments in the Act so that we should have greater freedom of action. But in the end we should still have a reproduction of the British constitution, less flexible because created by statute instead of by struggles, and always a copy, an imitation, not a genuine outgrowth of the Life of India, her Self-expression.

If the first alternative be accepted, all that Britain can do is to set India free to shape her own constitution, letting the present transitional form of Indo-British Government continue while India sets her own house in order, and frames her own constitution. The method would probably be by Provincial Conventions, and finally by a National Convention, in which would be worked out the Constitution of Provinces, and finally their Federation.

On such constitutions I have often written and spoken, in Addresses to District Conferences, to the National Congress, and I outline the scheme here.

What are the foundations laid in her past, which have preserved her through uncounted millennia, and which maintained her in such wealth and prosperity that all the merchants of Europe clamoured and struggled for the right to shake the eastern pagoda-tree? The answer may be given in a phrase: A system of Self-Government, beginning in the unit of the village, the "village republics," which remained, prosperous, well-to-do, and well-managed from the time that we meet them in the dawn of history to the second decade of the nineteenth century. These have gone with the Aryan race wherever its children have spread, and are still traceable in Europe, although practically robbed of their strength and beauty by the spread of feudalism. In India they lasted down to the nineteenth century, as just said. In Burma they lasted, with the same happy results down to the English conquest. For the happiness, prosperity, education and development of the masses of the people there is nothing comparable with them. In the Address presented to H.E. the Viceroy and the Rt. Hon. E. S. Montagu by the Home Rule Leagues we said:

> The argument that Democracy is foreign to India cannot be alleged by any well-informed person. Maine and other historians recognise the fact that Democratic Institutions are essentially Āryan, and spread from India to Europe with the immigration of Āryan peoples; Pañchāyaṭs, the "village republics," have been the most stable institution of India, and only vanished during the last century under the pressure of the East India Company's domination. They still exist within the castes, each caste forming within itself a thorough democracy, in which the same man may have as relations a prince and a peasant. Social rank does not depend so much on wealth and titles, as on learning and occupation. India is democratic in spirit, and in institutions left to her from the past and under her control in the present.

Home Rule Leagues may be said to be special pleaders. Then let Englishmen speak. Sir John Lawrence said as long ago as 1864:

> The people of India are quite capable of administering their own affairs, and the municipal

feeling is deeply rooted in them. The village communities, each of which is a little republic, are the most abiding of Indian institutions. Holding the position we do in India, every view of duty and policy should induce us to leave as much as possible of the business of the country to be done by the people.

Sir Bartle Frere, in 1871, wrote:

Any one who has watched the working of Indian society will see that its genius is one to represent, not merely by election under Reform Acts, but represent generally by provisions, every class of the community, and when there is any difficulty respecting any matter to be laid before Government, it should be discussed among themselves. When there is any fellow-citizen to be rewarded or punished, there is always a caste meeting, and this is an expression, it seems to me, of the genius of the people, as it was of the old Saxons, to gather together in assemblies of different types to vote by tribes or hundreds.

As Mr. Chisholm Anstey said:

We are apt to forget in this country, when we talk of preparing people in the East by education, and all that sort of thing, for Municipal Government and Parliamentary Government (if I may use such a term), that the East is the parent of Municipalities. Local Self-Government, in the widest acceptation of the term, is as old as the East itself. No matter what may be the religion of the people who inhabit what we call the East, there is not a portion of the country from west to east, from north to south, which is not swarming with municipalities, and not only so, but like to our municipalities of old, they are all bound together as in a species of network, so that you have ready-made to your hand the frame-work of a great system of representation.

Or let an Indian speak: Mr. C. P. Rāmaswāmi Aiyar, now Advocate-General of Madras, and member of the Provincial Legislative Council, said in his Presidential Address to the Second Malabar District Conference in 1917:

In Kauṭilya's *Arthashāsṭra*, Book III, Vol. 10, villagers are contemplated as constructing and maintaining in their corporate capacity works of public utility; and Professor Rhys Davids says: "Villagers are described in the Buḍḍhist books as uniting all their care to build mohallas and rest-houses, to mend the roads between their own and adjacent villages, and even to lay out parks." (*Vide* P. Bannerji's *Public Administration in Ancient India*, p. 293, note 2.) In Mysore, now, in many districts, the villagers give half a day's work free, per week, for works of public utility, and the aggregate value of the work done is astounding. Every village in the times of the *Arthashāsṭra*, (4th century B.C.) formed an integral part of the general administrative system and the village was the foundation of the Governmental edifice. The Village Government of those days partook not only of the administration of executive, but also of judiciary, functions, as will appear from the Ceylon inscriptions dealing with the administration of criminal justice of communal courts. To the credit of the Madras Government it must be said that, as against Sir T. Munro, who was a thorough individualist, the Madras Board of Revenue desired in the early years of the last century to leave the authority of the village institutions unimpaired. But Sir Thomas Munro had his way, and the village communities lost their vitality.

The Mysore Administration Report, 1915—16, explains the above allusion. It states that

> the villagers contributed Rs. 47,083 either in cash or in labour during the year, [the Government helping with grants amounting to Rs. 44,978]. The village committees continued to evince much interest in this work, and many works of public utility, such as construction of school buildings, sinking wells and opening roads, clearing lantana and planting trees, were carried out through their exertions throughout the State.

To this I added as comment:

> Conferences of the village committees were held in four districts, "to take stock of the work done by the committees, to discuss the needs and

requirements of the rural population, and to concert measures and draw up programmes for improving the economic and sanitary condition of the villages". The villagers fall in gladly with this communal work, which is on their traditional lines, giving definite amounts of free labour, as stated above, to the improvement of their village. The old sense of communal obligation still survives, and the Mysore Government has wisely utilised and fostered it.

In my *Lectures on Political Science*, delivered to students in the College of Commerce under the National University, I gave a detailed account with references to inscriptions and documents, describing the village and its constitution. They may be summarised thus:

The characteristics of the village were: a group of houses surrounded by a large tract of land, arable pasture and forest; each resident had a site free of rent for house, yard and garden. The establishment consisted of the officers and craftsmen, whose services were free to all, and who were given land, and various other rights to shares of produce, as remuneration. These consisted of a headman, an accountant, a watchman, who also discharged some police functions, a boundary-man, a superintendent of tanks and watercourses, a pūjāri, a school master, an astrologer, a doctor, a musician, a poet, a dancing girl, a barber, a washerman, a cow-keeper, a potter, a smith and a carpenter. The village assembly the Pañchāyaṭ, governed, elected by "pot-tickets," or otherwise, and formed committees for branches of work; in the fact that the village rulers were elected lay the safety of the village; when the Company changed election to appointment, they became village tyrants.

The Decentralisation Committee's Report said (§ 736):

> We consider that as Local Self-Government should commence in the villages with the establishment of Village Pañchāyaṭs, so the next step should be the constitution of boards for areas of smaller size than a district. We desire therefore, to see sub-district boards universally established as the principal agencies of rural board associations.

Speaking at a District Conference on this matter, I said on the establishment of Pañchāyaṭs:

Village needs would thus be made known, and if necessary they could be represented by the Pañchāyaṭ to a higher authority. The village would become articulate through its Pañchāyaṭ, and would no longer be the dumb and often driven creature which it is to-day. And it would be brought into touch with the larger life. The Pañchāyaṭ might invite lecturers, organise discussions, arrange amusements, games, etc. All village life would be lifted to a higher level, widened and enriched by such organisation, and each village, further, forming one of a group of villages, would realise its unity with others, and thus become an organ of the larger corporate life.

The corresponding unit in the Towns to the Village in the country is the Ward, and the Ward Pañchāyaṭ, like the Village one, should be elected by Household Suffrage. All towns with populations over 5,000 should have Ward Pañchāyaṭs under control of the Municipality. Below that population, a Ward Pañchāyaṭ would be the only municipal authority. These Ward Councils should take up the smaller town matters, now neglected, because the Municipality is too heavily burdened to attend to them properly. The elementary Schools in each

Ward should be in its charge; scavenging and sanitation generally, and care for the cleanliness of the streets and latrines; provision and superintendence of stands for hire vehicles and resting carts, with water-troughs for horses and cattle; the inspection of foodstuffs and prevention of adulteration; arbitration in small disputes as in France —where so much litigation is prevented by the appointment of a small tradesman as a local judge—inspection of workshops, wells, etc.—all these matters would naturally fall into the hands of the Ward Councils. Where there is a Municipality, that body would delegate to the Ward Councils such matters as it thought fit.

The land was communal property and redistributed from time to time. All householders appear to have had votes, forfeited for crimes, but certain qualifications were laid down for eligibility for election as a Pañchā (Councillor). Women were eligible as well as men. Careful rules are laid down in the books for the buildings of a village, the planting of flowering trees in its roads, and trees for timber on the outskirts, etc. Outcastes, employed as labourers, were provided for, they had houses, yards, and the general village privileges. The wealth of India lay in her villages; and in wars between different kingdoms, often for purposes of annexation, the villages were respected, since the would-be ruler had to depend on them largely for his income. A portion of the land in kingdoms was set apart for the King in exchange for his protection, and the produce belonged to him; or he was assigned a share—a fourth, a sixth, a twelfth, of each crop. The duty of the village was production and trade, the duty of the soldier was to fight; and battles were carried on by armies, we read, within sight of unmolested peasants at the plough. Raiders from beyond the frontier robbed and devastated to some extent, but serious invaders carried away great wealth, mostly of jewels and the precious metals which, after all, interfered little with the amenities of the village life.

After the village unit came a group of villages, then a larger group of these groups, and so on. In Kingdoms and Empires, Governments were based on similar models; in the great Empire of Chanḍraguptạ I, his Council was made up of the Pañchāyaṭ of each department in his Government; so in the Municipal Council of a city.

The successive enlarging areas of Government still exist; there is the Village; the group of Villages or Taluq; the group of Taluqs or District; the group of Districts, or Province; the group of Provinces, or Nation. The vote in the successive enlarging areas should depend on the enlarging knowledge, and eligibility to Councils on higher education, or experience in government by membership of a lower grade of Council, and perhaps on a minimum age. Membership in a Council might be a qualification for a vote in the electorate of a higher Council. The aim should be to let knowledge give power; every man or woman who was a major should have a vote for a Village Pañchāyaṭ or a Town Pañchāyaṭ (Ward Council); they know village wants, which are their own. The vote for a Taluq Council should demand an educational qualification or membership in a Village Pañchāyaṭ, and so on.

An additional vote might be acquired by special qualifications, or by exceptional services. In this way a Provincial Council would include, if possible consist of, the best men in the Province, save those sent on to the National Parliament.

Politics is a Science and an Art, the most difficult of all, and the welfare of all parts of the Nation is concerned with, is affected by, the interdependence of all. Yet men and women vote for a member, say, of a British Parliament who cannot judge by his or her knowledge of his fitness to decide the questions on which the welfare of the Nation depends.

It is as though the cabinboys elected the captain of the ship.

In connection with the grades of Councils would be arranged the ascending series of schools under their control from the elementary to the University; also the guidance of agriculture, the provision of suitable seeds, manures, animals for breeding, model farms, agricultural colleges for research; in fact all the organisations needed for prosperity, and bringing the results of the knowledge of experts within reach of the cultivators, the craftsmen, the producers of every kind. The whole National life would be invigorated by a system built by Indian genius on the foundations laid in India's past, to which her children would respond.

These are, of course, but suggestions, offered for discussion, but they are enough to show why I think India should form her own constitution, and not blindly adopt a constitution made in England.

The Conventions, spoken of on p. 279 in the second paragraph, should be composed, say, of members elected to the new Councils at the end of 1923, and of any special persons, co-opted by them. This should be borne in mind in the choosing of members. They would sit in the Councils for their ordinary legislative work. They would take part in a Convention outside that work, co-opt persons whose help they desired, and work out the new legislative scheme.

CHAPTER IX

IN A WORLD-COMMONWEALTH OR ALONE?

WE come finally to the question: Shall India become an isolated and independent country, or shall she remain as part of a world-wide Empire, or better, as part of a world-wide Commonwealth, of Free Nations?

That question can only be answered by India herself, and none can dictate to any Nation its decision, or say what, in the future, shall be the decision of posterity. But denying as I do, and as I must—believing in the value of Nationhood—that any Nation has the right to impose by force its authority on any other Nation, and therefore admitting also the right of any Nation to throw off such authority imposed upon it, either with or without the consent of the foreign Nation, I would most strongly and earnestly pray both India and Britain to remain linked hand-in-hand, for the good of the world, for the sake of Humanity in the present, and still more in the future. Looking back on the conflict between the Nations of Europe which went on through the eighteenth century between European Nations, represented by their Mercantile Companies, and the final triumph of Britain over its rivals (see Introduction), for, as I believe, the reason given on p. 11, I think that that view, published in 1915, has been proved true by the widening of Freedom since the Crown assumed authority in 1858, until now we stand close to the attainment of Home Rule, the "inevitable result" of the connection. Again, the unique way in which the Company, aiming only at trade advantages, built itself into a Governing Power, and was justly overthrown for its tyrannies and annexations by the Sepoy Rebellion—the annexation of Ouḍh being the match which fired the mine of Indian discontent—so that the whole of its ill-gotten authority passed to the Crown, all this pointed to the same conclusion. That Crown, again, was changed from a Royal into an Imperial one by Benjamin Disraeli, a Hebrew, who with Oriental imagination, envisaged the change which had come over the position of Britain by the bringing under her rule, as Lord Paramount, as Chakravarṭi, the mighty Empire which reproduced the earlier Empires of Chanḍragupṭa, of Ashoka, of others as far-flung, that had emphasised from time to time in the past the geographical, as well as the religious and cultural, unity of India. Nor is it without significance, that, after India had awakened again into Self-consciousness as a Nation, largely as a result of English literature so strangely coupled with un-English bureaucracy—the twain working in the same direction, like the Suras and Asuras turning Mount Meru—the one stimulative, the other repressive, forcing the hopes and aspirations from fluidity into solidity, that when the time had come it was an Oriental, a Hebrew, who, as Secretary of State, shaped the mould for the coming Home Rule, proclaimed as Britain's goal in India; then a third Oriental—again a member of that wondrous race which gave birth to a Christ whom the West worships, and which has survived the most ghastly twenty centuries of the uttermost cruelty that the world has seen—a third Hebrew, should be placed on the Viceregal Throne, perhaps, as we hope, to complete Indian Home Rule. Nor must we omit one world-change, which has prevented the English from settling down in India as did the Pathāns and Mughals, and becoming a type distinguishable, but Indian, as did those;

it was the immense change brought about by swift intercommunication between all parts of the world, so that distances were time-shortened, and, ere long, will become shorter than the grandfathers of present-day England took to travel from Land's End to John o'Groats. I cannot look back over the three centuries and ten years from 1612 to 1922, and miss the golden thread of a divine purpose in bringing under one Crown the root-stock and the youngest sub-race of the Āryan Race.

Is not that purpose that these two may be joined in an Indo-British Commonwealth, composed of coloured and of white Nations, of Asiatics and Europeans, of Easterns and Westerns, of Religion and Applied Science, forming a model, making certain the realisation, of a World Federation, wherein Justice shall reign instead of Power, and Law shall put an end to Violence?

Shall India make that Vision come true, or shall she reject her glorious opportunity and choose isolation and—decay?

That is the question to which we must now address ourselves.

I submit that India, independent and alone, will recommence the old story of invasions and subjections, and must at once begin to prepare for these by increasing her huge military expenditure in preparation for the near withdrawal not only of British troops, but of the great protection of Britain's mighty name. As part of a great Commonwealth, the strength of the whole Commonwealth is her defence. As she rushed to the defence of Britain, overmatched in Europe, so would the Nations of the Commonwealth rush to hers, if she were attacked from outside. Britain's navy is still the largest in the world, and that navy will be a sister-guardian of her long coast-line, even after she has created a navy of her own. All the strength of the Commonwealth will be at the call of every Nation in it, and that knowledge is sufficient to protect. In mere numbers, China is the only country that matches the Commonwealth, and in organisation, in effectiveness for self-defence, there is no comparison between the two.

Nor can we leave out of account, in thinking of an independent India, the fact that one-third of her area is occupied by Indian States, which, with the cessation of the British Overlordship would become independent kingdoms, as of yore. Many of them have well-trained troops and full treasuries. In a Home Rule India, these States would be autonomous units, and it may be that the Council of Princes might form a part of the Parliament of India. But in an Independent India, a desire to remove their neighbour's landmarks would probably arise, and the New India might have to defend her freedom against the aggressiveness of the armed major States, while she was still incapable of armed defence.

Another serious question arises with regard to the Muhammadans of India. If the relation between Muslims and Hindūs were as it was in the Lucknow days, this question would not be so urgent, though it would even then have almost certainly arisen, sooner or later, in an Independent India. But since the Khilāfaṭ agitation, things have changed, and it has been one of the many injuries inflicted on India by the encouragement of the Khilāfaṭ crusade, that the inner Muslim feeling of hatred against "unbelievers" has sprung up, naked and unashamed, as in years gone by. We have seen revived, as guide in practical politics, the old Muslim religion of the sword; we have seen the dragging out of centuries of forgetfulness the old exclusiveness, claiming the Jazirut-ul-Arab—the Island of Arabia—as a Holy Land which may not be trodden by the polluting foot of a non-Muslim; we have heard Muslim leaders declare that if the Afghāns invaded India, they would join their fellow-believers, and would slay the Hindūs who defended their Motherland against the foe; we have been forced to see that the primary allegiance of Musalmāns is to Islāmic countries, not to our Motherland; we have learned that their dearest hope is to establish the "kingdom of God," not God as Father of the world, loving all His creatures, but as a God seen through Musalmān spectacles, resembling in His commands—through one of the Prophets, as to the treatment of unbelievers—the Mosaic JHVH of the early Hebrews, when they were fighting, as did the early Muslims, for freedom to follow the religion given to them by their Prophet. The world has gone beyond such so-called Theocracies, in which "God's" commands are given through a man. The claim now put forward by

Musalmān leaders that they must obey the laws of their particular Prophet above the laws of the State in which they live, is subversive of civic order and the stability of the State; it makes them bad citizens, for their centre of allegiance is outside the Nation, and they cannot, while they hold the views proclaimed by Moulanas Muhammad Ali and Shaukat Ali—to name the most prominent of these Muslim leaders—be trusted by their fellow-citizens. If India were independent, the Muslim part of the population—for the ignorant masses would follow those who appealed to them in the name of their Prophet—would become an immediate peril to India's freedom. Allying themselves with Afghānisṭān, Beluchisṭān, Persia, Irāq, Arabia, Turkey and Egypt, and with such of the tribes of Central Asia who are Musalmāns, they would rise to place India under the rule of Islām—those in (now) "British India" being helped by the Muslim Indian States—and would establish Musalmān rule. We had thought that Indian Musalmāns were loyal to their Motherland, and, indeed, we still hope that some of the educated class might strive to prevent such a Musalmān rising; but they are too few for effective resistance, and would be murdered as apostates. Malabar has taught us what Islāmic rule still means, and we do not want to see another specimen of the "Khilāfaṭ Rāj" in India. How much sympathy with the Moplas is felt by Muslims outside Malabar has been proved by the defence raised for them by their fellow-believers, and by Mr. Gandhi himself, who stated that they had acted as they believed that their religion taught them to act. I fear that that is true; but there is no place in a civilised land for people who believe that their religion teaches them to murder, rob, rape, burn, or drive away out of the country those who refuse to apostatise from their ancestral faiths, except in its schools, under surveillance, or in its gaols. The Thugs believed that their particular form of God commanded them to strangle people—especially travellers with money. Such "laws of God" cannot be allowed to override the laws of a civilised country, and people living in the twentieth century must either educate people who hold these Middle Age views, or else exile them. Their place is in countries sharing their opinions, where they can still use such arguments against any who differ from them—as indeed, Persia did with the Pārsīs long ago, and the Bahaists in our own time. In fact, Muslim sects are not safe in a country ruled by orthodox Muslims. British rule in India has protected the freedom of all sects: Shiahs, Sunnis, Sūfis, Bahaists, live in safety under her sceptre, although it cannot protect any of them from social ostracism, where it is in a minority; Musalmāns are more free under British rule, than in countries where there are Muslim rulers. In thinking of an Independent India, the menace of Muhammadan rule has to be considered.

To break the British connection would mean not Freedom but only a change of masters, for Japan is armed *cap à pied*, her population is over-crowded and needs an outlet; India, at present, cannot defend herself alone, and Japan would seize the hour of her weakness. To declare Independence now would be madness, and Britain would not be foolish enough to protect, while Independent India was preparing for future self-defence. She would either clear out at once, and leave India to be overrun, or would try to hold her down by force, while encouraging dissensions among her people, to the ultimate ruin of both great countries. For, without India, Britain would fall from her position as the greatest of World-Powers, while with India, and possibly re-linked with the

United States in close alliance, she would lead the forward evolution of Humanity for centuries to come.

The word "Empire" has had evil connotations, for it has always been connected with military conquest, the subjugation of other countries, and autocratic rule. Old people will remember the bitter opposition which arose in India when Disraeli proposed that Queen Victoria should assume the title of Empress of India. And so strong and so angry was it, that the title was only permitted to be attached to India, "a subject country". Great Britain would have none of it. Victoria, Edward VII, George V have remained Royal, not Imperial, outside India. Our reigning Monarch is King of Great Britain and Ireland, of the Dominions Overseas, and of all Crown Colonies and Possessions; he is Emperor in India only, and the title marks out the difference between India and the rest of the Nations who own his sway. Everywhere else he is a constitutional King; here he has been an autocratic Emperor, though inconsistently ruling through Ministers, responsible to Parliament in Britain. Now that he has proclaimed that "Swarāj has begun" in India, the incongruous name of Emperor should disappear, and Empire would follow it. "Free Nations" in an Empire is unhistorical, and the Prince of Wales acted in the spirit of Freedom when he preferred to use the word "Commonwealth," rather than the word "Empire". He was moved by a true instinct. To be the acknowledged Head of a "Commonwealth of Free Nations" is a magnificent position. To be an "Emperor" does not call up in memory names one desires to remember. We may note, in passing, that the Hungarians, in whom the feeling for Liberty is strong, refused to acknowledge allegiance to the Emperor of Austria; they crowned him as King of Hungary. It is not without interest that the German

Empire, embodying the ideas of an autocratic Emperor, of military domination, of the imposition on a conquered world of the German ideals of the State and of "Kultur," was destroyed by the War. Let the dead thing go, in name as well as in reality, and let us have in its place the voluntary assent of Free Nations to enter into partnership for mutual helpfulness, and for their strength to be used in the service of the world. Much of the instinctive objection among Indians to the "Empire" is due to this perhaps unconscious prejudice against the word, and the difference of status implied in its application to their country alone. "Commonwealth" sounds sweet in their ears. To enter into a "Commonwealth of Free Nations" is more attractive than to enter into an Empire. So I shall use the word Commonwealth here. As a recognition of the fact that India represents Asia, that the coloured races rank with the white, that her population is far greater than that of all the other countries put together, that it is the nucleus of a future World-Commonwealth, the best title would be the "Indo-British Commonwealth".

Now, why should India enter, as an equal partner, into this great and unique Federation? I think that the fundamental reason is that we see a tendency in evolution to bring about aggregations of separate entities into organic wholes, each embodying and directed by a Life of a higher grade of unfoldment, and that it is wiser to work with the Law than against it. The smallest individual recognised by Science is a plastid, *i.e.*, an unwalled fragment of matter, able to exist alone, and showing the functions which are regarded as those of "life". It is quite independent, except that it requires for its continued existence an environment which supplies air, liquid and solid particles. The cell is next formed, with a wall as a limit; cells are aggregated into tissues and organs, forming bodies; these into families, tribes, small Nations, each, biologically, an individual in the ascending grades. The Nations blend into larger Nations, a Heptarchy into England, separate States into Kingdoms, Republics, organised wholes. The States of New South Wales, Victoria, etc., unite into the Commonwealth of Australia. Each larger organisation evolves larger interests. As each of the scattered units of British "possessions" won freedom of individualised, or National, life, it became a component part of the "British Empire," a son coming of age, as it were, having his own family but remaining part of a larger family, held by ties of blood and custom. That process is going on, and the time has come for India to have her own household again under her own control, and to have her status acknowledged as that of a mature member of the larger household. The Commonwealth is a "joint family system," and that Commonwealth needs the synthesising genius of India, and her binding sense of obligation of each to each, and of all to the whole. We have to reconcile the liberty of each with the liberty of all, to solve on a higher level the recurring problem of the liberty of the individual human unit and of the collections of individuals as parts of a larger individual, the Nation to their Liberty, and their mutual relations. As the organs to the body, so are classes, castes, communities to their Nation; their rightful liberty of functioning is necessary to the life of the Nation, and the excesses of that liberty cause the diseases of the Nation, and consequent restlessness, irritability, disturbances, like the diseases of any other individual, when his organs suffer from over-depletion or over-fulness. Mutual harmony is the law for healthy life and consequent happiness. No Nation is complete and perfect within itself; in a Society of Nations lives a higher and fuller Life, and the great new Individual of this embryo Commonwealth needs the addition of India, a Nation, for the mutual benefit of herself and of all the rest. Alone, India will be less great than as an organ in the larger body, animated by a higher unfoldment of the One Life. As the life in an individual man is less than the life in a Nation, so is the life in Federated Nations greater than the life in any one of them. Into such a Federation may India enter, if she will.

Obviously, there are many advantages in such an entry, both for the world and for herself.

For the world it means Peace. The danger of war between the coloured and the white races would disappear, a war which would lay desolate the world. It would also mean peace from wars between single Nations, for the Indo-British Commonwealth would be the mightiest Power in the world, and would be able, through the instrumentality of the League of Nations, to substitute arbitration for war. For the coloured races it would mean Justice and Safety, by the amity of both in a world-wide Brotherhood. It would exercise a constant gentle pressure upon all outside it to unite in appropriate aggregations, with a view to a later World-Commonwealth, while offering an example of the advantages of diversity in unity for mutual advantage. It would mean a blending of opposites as complementaries instead of as rivalries, of the right adjustment of duties and rights, of authority and liberty. It would mean, through India, the spiritualisation of National life, and thereby the most splendid example the world has yet seen of Progress in obedience to Law, and within the limits of Order.

And what would it mean to India herself, in addition to these world gains? It would mean internal peace, and safety from external aggressions. It would mean the glory of leading the world towards spirituality, and of showing to all the way to intellectual splendour, to higher Art, to physical prosperity, for she proved in her earlier life that these were the fruits of a civilisation, based on spiritual Wisdom, and they decayed as that highest form of life was obscured. In the Indo-British Commonwealth it would regain a worthy embodiment, and would shine out in more than its ancient splendour and beauty.

Before our eyes rises a Vision of dazzling glory. The India and Britain types of Religion and Applied Science, walk hand-in-hand, leading the long procession of the Nations of the world, clad in the white robes of Spirit, with the golden and jewelled ornaments of material prosperity. Their heads are crowned with diamond-studded circlets of Knowledge, and in their hands they carry the symbols of Arts, the instruments of Crafts, the emblems of Commerce and of Industry. Earth's happy children play in front and beside them, scattering flowers in their way, and Heaven's children rain on them from the shining skies the blossoms gathered in the flowering meads of their own brighter world.

By mutual love, by mutual trust and confidence, forgetting all the sorrows that lie behind, and reaching forward to the glad destiny offered to the twain together, but to neither separately, let us go hand-in-hand and work for the realisation of that destiny, fairer than aught the elder world has seen. Let us waste no more time in quarrelling over the past. Let us march onward and create the future.

PEACE TO ALL BEINGS

APPENDICES

THESE two Appendices show that the claim then was the same as the claim now, except that the latter is regarded as nearer its fulfilment than was then thought possible, because of the quickening action of the war on the world-environment of India.

THE following is from a pamphlet, *Self-Government for India*, published in 1915.

Here we come, at last, to the bedrock of our claim for Self-Government. India is a Nation, and in Nationhood is included the natural, inherent, indefeasible right to Self-Government. No one civilised Nation can permanently keep another civilised Nation in bondage; Egypt is said to have tried it with Israel, but the results were not encouraging, even though the civilisation and the wisdom of Egypt were incomparably higher than those of the Hebrews. The claim of Great Britain to decide when and how far India will be "fit for Self-Government" is a piece of arrogance that would be intolerable, were it not so naively unconscious. Let England think what she would feel if, owing to internal dissensions, the Chinese had invaded her, and had conquered her with the help of a large part of her own population. If, thereafter, all the Government of the country were in Chinese hands; if they themselves were deprived of arms;

shut out of the higher posts in their own army and navy; not allowed to volunteer in defence of their own coasts; the Prime Minister and all his Cabinet Chinese; the Lord Chancellor a Chinaman; all the higher offices filled by Chinese; all the Education shaped by Chinese; the money raised by taxation used to make strategic railways, while education was starved, and the masses left illiterate; examinations to fill posts in England held in China; the taxes on Christians used to pay Buḍḍhist priests and to encourage Buḍḍhist education and Buḍḍhist propaganda; compelled to learn Chinese in order to hold the subordinate offices open to them; looked down upon by the Chinese as an inferior race, and treated as foreigners in their own country. Would *they* be contented? would *they* never aspire towards freedom? would there be no "unrest" in England under such conditions?

"Do Indians feel like that?" a Civilian Judge once asked me, quite surprised. "They feel just like that," I answered. "It never struck me in that way," he replied thoughtfully. And that is so. It never strikes them. They honestly feel that they are ruling India so much better than Indians could rule it. None the less does a Nation prefer being even badly ruled by itself to being well ruled by benevolent foreigners. Moreover, we have above pointed out some advantages of Self-Rule.

O English Nation! Great and free and proud. Cannot you see? Cannot you understand? Cannot you realise that your Indian brothers feel now as you would feel then? That to be a stranger in your own country, an alien in your own land, with no rights save those given by the grace of a Government not your own, your inferiority taken for granted, your capacities weighed in alien scales, and measured by the wand of another Nation—you could not bear such a state, such an outlook. India is patient, as you would not be. She does not want to break the link; she wants to remain part of the Empire; but an equal part, a Self-Governing Community, standing on a level with the Self-Governing Dominions. Is this passionate longing, sedition? Is this ineradicable hope, treason? You dare not say so, you who bred Hampden, and Sidney, and Milton, you whose glory is your Freedom, you who boast of your Empire as an Empire of the Free. Who dared to ask if you were fit for freedom? Charles I asked it. James II asked it. History records the answer that you gave.

Is India fit for Freedom? She claims it as her Right. You will not say her, Nay. She proved her equality in death on the battle-field. Will you refuse it when the peace she has made possible, broods over your homes? Would they have been as safe from the German, if Indian breasts had not formed part of your shield?

What does India want? She wants everything that any other Nation may claim for itself. To be free in India, as the Englishman is free in England. To be governed by her own men, freely elected by herself. To make and break Ministries at her will. To carry arms; to have her own army, her own navy, her own volunteers. To levy her own taxes; to make her own budgets; to educate her own people; to irrigate her own lands; to mine her own ores; to mint her own coin; to be a Sovereign Nation within her own borders, owning the paramount power of the Imperial Crown, and sending her sons to the Imperial Council. There is nothing to which any man can aspire in his own land from which the Indian must be shut out here.

A large claim, you say. Does the Englishman ask less for himself in England? If yes, what is there strange that an Indian should ask the same for himself in India? What is the radical difference between them which should make an Indian *content* to be a thrall? It is not the "angle of vision" that needs changing. It is the eye, purified from pride and prejudice, that can see clearly, and the heart, purged from arrogance, that can beat with healthy strokes.

England and India hand-in-hand. Yes, that is our hope, for the world's sake. But that it may be so, Justice must replace inequality; for India can never be at rest, till she is free.

II

THE following is from a pamphlet, *Home Rule and the Empire*, a lecture delivered in 1916.

Now, I have said that India has a right to Home Rule, like the Self-Governing Dominions of the Empire. But I am not the first to say it, although the particular phrase "Home Rule" has caught the popular fancy. The Congress has been saying it year after year during its splendid life, and you remember how in 1906 when the Grand Old Man of India, Dadabhai Naoroji, came out of his retirement to be President of the Calcutta Congress, too feeble to read his own speech so that another read it for him, he yet read the words which claimed Swarāj—Self-Rule—and the crowd leapt up and echoed "Swarāj". It chanced that a year ago I used the words "Home Rule" instead of Self-Government. The first is shorter: *Self-Government* is four syllables and *Home Rule* only two. For a popular cry a short name is better than a long one. Moreover, it was a more explicit phrase, because Self-Government might mean independence, and so, to show you did not mean a break between Great Britain and India, it was necessary to add "within the Empire," and so you have a great mouthful "Self-Government within the Empire on Colonial lines". I prefer to call it *Home Rule*. The advantage is that it is a cry for Freedom without separation. Home Rule does not mean that England and India ought to be torn apart. It means only that India shall be mistress in her own household. Home Rule has been given to Ireland, although the Act is hung up in a way that an Act was never hung up before. Still it is on the Statute Book, and so Home Rule is now a most respectable phrase. When a modern scientist rediscovered what we used to call mesmerism, he called it hypnotism. Mesmerism was discredited because the first man who discovers a thing is always called a quack. When another man finds it out, he gives it a new label, and then it becomes respectable in polite society. I baptised this movement with the name of Home Rule, because Home Rule had been admitted to and had gone through the House of Commons, and was made into law. To my astonishment, I find it is the most disreputable thing to say. Yet I read in *The Madras Times* that Home Rule is inevitable, and that every one who looked at it saw that it must come: the only thing was that it must not come in a hurry.

We are not asking for it until the reconstruction of the Empire takes place, and that is a matter of a very considerable number of years. All we are asking now is that we may be allowed to educate the people in a constitutional and law-abiding way, so that when the reconstruction of the Empire comes, India may be ready, as the Colonies are getting ready to-day—a modest enough request.

I am told that some people believe that I desire separation. Friends, I have been speaking in India now for three-and-twenty years. My first lecture was given in the Madras Presidency when I visited your larger Madras towns, and that was in 1893. We are now in 1916. In those first lectures of mine I spoke strongly in favour of maintaining the union between Great Britain and India, and from that day to this I have never wavered in that belief. I have taught year after year that the welfare of both Nations is bound up in their union, that England and India together can do what neither England nor India separated could ever do, and that their union is God-prepared and God-given. How often have I lectured, showing how the different European Nations came here, how the Dutch came, how the Portuguese came, how the French came, and how at last the English came, and England was the only one that came to remain and to build up a mighty Empire that is the wonder of the world? England with her practical ability, with her business strength, with her scientific knowledge, with her practical brain is the complement of India spiritual, philosophical and somewhat lacking nowadays in the qualities that are pre-eminently British. It has not always been so. There was a day when to be an Indian was to be full of energy, full of life, full of power, where the Kṣhaṭṭriyas of India were soldiers who had not their match for courage and for chivalry in any Nation of the world. It may be that in courage a German is as good as a Rājpuṭ, but the Rājpuṭ's courage was in his own heart while the courage of the German is in the battalion. He would never ride out as Rājpuṭs rode out one by one until they fell dead on the battlefield, too proud to yield, too gallant to submit. This modern idea of the "mild Hinḍū," as they say, is a very modern idea, and it goes with the great mistake that had been made in India some years ago—the same mistake as is made by some people in England—that the teaching that is given to the Sannyāsin was meant to be a teaching given to every one at large. You have forgotten the old Āshramas. All men speak as if they were going to be guided by the teaching of the Sannyâsin while they cling to power, gold and the interests of the daily life of man. Hypocrite is the man who claims to say: "I am Brahman," and yet is a slave to the lusts of the flesh. So, with that failure in her religion and with the loss of spirituality, India lost the courage, strength and vigour of the earlier days. India to-day is misjudged and is thought to be a Nation of visionaries so that all the other Nations of the world may plunder her. But the old spirit lives in India still. A century and a half of foreign rule does not suffice to break the spirit of India, and when the word went out calling on her to learn self-respect once more, when Hinḍūism was held up even by the foreigner as the noblest and the sublimest religion that had come to man, when from one end of the country to another her ancient religion revived and the other great religions of the past began to reappear, when the Buḍḍhist began to hold up his head instead of being ashamed of his religion, then it was that the breath of new life breathed through India and she woke from the slumber of one hundred and fifty years. It was hard work—the reawakening of India. But now that India is awake, England ought to realise it for the sake of the Empire, for India's Home Rule would be England's salvation. Then and then only will she have the primacy of Asia, and then and then only will she be able to hold her own against China and Japan, and guard her Colonies and realise that her wide Empire is really a unit, united heart and soul. For England's sake, were I pleading her cause, I should ask for Indian Home Rule, for then, India would become the buttress of the Empire, and there would be no more distrust of Indians, for they would be the greatest citizens that the world has known. I hold that there is no Nation greater and nobler than Britain in her age-long assertion of liberty, and she has won for herself in modern days the place of the Mother of Liberty. I can never forget the childhood's memory when sitting, looking down on the crowds that filled the streets, I saw an opening out of the crowd as the carriage came along, and in it, standing up, the red-shirted Garibaldi, the Saviour of Italy. That was after Mazzini was an exile from Italy, when no country in the world save England opened her doors to call the Italian exile in. I remember that England also sheltered Prince Kropotkin, and sheltered Stepniak, the man of the Red Terror, vowed to assassinate the Tsar of Russia. Fugitives of liberty all the world over came to that little Island, and in that little Island they found a peaceful home;

and for the sake of the world's rebellions, for the sake of the world's heroes and martyrs and exiles, England's name shall ever shine in Liberty's sky as one of the brightest stars that shine therein. I cannot forget it all, although I am not English but Irish. But for the sake of those old memories, I would fain that India had Home Rule—it will make that little Island of Liberty safe.

Again, I must remind you that Home Rule is absolutely necessary for the sake of the youth of India, for India's younger generation are being mis-educated, misled and mistrained under the education that they are receiving. Those lads in College and those boys in School are full of unrest and discontent, breaking now and then into those unhappy strikes which no lover of students can sanction. The boys are helpless, and many ruin their whole lives in the madness of the moment. But those boys in England would be the pride of their Nation, high-spirited, self-respecting, and they would be cherished as the future heroes of their native land; for the self-respect of a boy is a precious possession, and if you kill it in the heart of the boy, it is hard to revive it in the heart of the man when the boy has come into man's estate. Why is it that Indian boys are told that they should be so submissive, should behave in a way which is against all Indian tradition of boyish thought and feeling? The men who made England's Empire were not good obedient boys—they were "bad boys" like Clive, naughty, troublesome and rebellious, because they were strong and vigorous. The "docility" of Indian students is due to an overworked brain and under-nourished body, and the sooner the educational authorities recognise that, the better it will be for our boys. The Indian tradition, for boys who are not to be teachers, is one of vigour, manliness, martial spirit, strong bodies, dexterous in arms, in horsemanship, in all exercises. Their Gurus encouraged their virility and pride of race, they did not try to cow them. The broken-spirited boy is the cringing subservient man. We must have Home Rule for the sake of our boys.

We must have Home Rule for the sake of our women, before they are denationalised and despiritualised by a mongrel education. Two great classes of Indians are marked down as "illiterate," our women and our raiyats. Yet both of these may be said to be intellectually literate, though they may not be able to read and write, for they understand the great problems of human life and the sublime teachings of the Hinḍū religion, better than many of their would-be teachers.

It is a greater thing to be educated in life than to be educated in books. We want Home Rule in order that India may have the kind of education that Indians require and that only Indians can give.

We want Home Rule in order that India may have economic freedom, so that her dying industries may be revived. How can you be prosperous when you have no control over your own finances? If you had control over your finances, you would largely increase your irrigation works and you would spend less money on railways, and insist on reasonable freight charges. The protection of industries in India is based on a topsy-turvy system. Here we have the English Government protecting the industries of German manufacturers and of Lancashire manufacturers against Indian manufacturers. They give concessions to foreign companies to exploit your lands.

It is not only these considerations that make me desire Home Rule for India, but it is also because I know that the Indian character is priceless to the world, that it is unique in its characteristics. It is a character so strong and yet so loving, so powerful in will and yet so gentle, and that character will never grow to its full stature until an Indian is a free man in a free country. As. Mr. Gokhale said, we are asking for India what every free Nation has —that an Indian may be in India what an Englishman is in England, and what a Frenchman is in France; may feel that he is a citizen of the British Empire, may realise that he has a splendid birthright which he will hand on to the generations that will come after him in the days to come, holding up his head, speaking out his thought, and never softening it for fear of what the Government may do.

Friends, is it not true that while you sympathise with me in heart, you dare not say so openly, for fear of the officials? I do not blame you. Every man cannot be a hero. You have wives and little children, and your children look to you for bread, and your wife looks to you for the food of the children dearer to her than her own life. Dare I blame you then?

I desire Home Rule for India because I love India and Indians as I love no other country, no other race on earth; because all dearest memories of the past are bound up for me with this Nation, and not with other peoples. I went to the West to take this white body, because it is more useful to

India, because it gives me strength to plead, and because it gives more weight to what I say—even with you, alas, the words from a white mouth have a little more influence; not so much now, thank God, but it was so when I first came here—and because of that, I—knowing that many of you will do to-morrow that which for the moment is not wrong but is dangerous—I say all this. To stand for freedom against autocracy is a dangerous thing; but more and more people are coming forward and speaking out, and expressing readiness to sacrifice their means and their careers for the sake of India. I believe that more and more are desirous to give themselves up for the Motherland; and this I know, that if in this great battle for Home Rule I go down, where I fall, a thousand will rise to carry on the struggle for freedom. When a Nation is once resolute to be free, there is no power on earth nor in heaven that can keep her back from freedom.

INDEX

PAGE PAGE